INTRODUCING
JESUS

INTRODUCING
JESUS

A Short Guide to the Gospels'
History and Message

Mark L. Strauss

 ZONDERVAN®

ZONDERVAN

Introducing Jesus
Copyright © 2018 by Mark L. Strauss

This title is also available as a Zondervan ebook.

Requests for information should be addressed to:
Zondervan, 3900 *Sparks Dr. SE, Grand Rapids, Michigan 49546*

ISBN 978-0-310-52858-6

Cover photo: 123RF, Masterfile
Interior design: Denise Froehlich

Printed in the United States of America

18 19 20 21 22 /DHV/ 10 9 8 7 6 5 4 3 2 1

CONTENTS

PREFACE

This book is an introduction to the life and ministry of Jesus of Nazareth, the most influential person who ever lived. Jesus has been the topic of more books, movies, discussions, and debates than any person in human history. Even our calendar is dated from the beginning of his life! Millions have dedicated their lives to serving him. Countless thousands have died as martyrs for his cause.

But who was this Jesus? To understand Jesus, we have to understand the New Testament Gospels, which are the primary source documents for his life and ministry. Where did these books come from? Why were they written? What can they tell us about Jesus? Are they historically reliable? For Christian believers, the Gospels narrate the climax and turning point of human history, when God acted decisively through Jesus the Messiah to achieve salvation for people everywhere. Even to those who do not follow Jesus as their Lord, the Gospels serve as our most important source of information for this profoundly important person. To study the Gospels is to study the origins of a faith and a movement that changed the world forever.

This book is an abridgement and condensation of my textbook *Four Portraits, One Jesus: A Survey of Jesus and the Gospels.* In it we will discuss the nature of the Gospels (chap. 1), survey their historical and religious backgrounds (chaps. 2–3), introduce each Gospel, including its themes and theology (chaps. 4–11), and examine a variety of questions related to the historical Jesus (chaps. 12–19). Two appendixes discuss some of the more technical questions related to Gospel methodologies.

My hope is that this brief introduction will spark greater interest in the person of Jesus Christ and in the inspired volumes that tell his story.

CHAPTER 1

WHAT ARE THE GOSPELS?

Many years ago when my oldest son was two years old, we took him to a portrait studio to have his picture taken. Two-year-olds are a bundle of emotions, and getting them to sit still through a photo shoot is a real challenge. During that short session, my son went through a range of moods, from contentment, to laughter, to pouting, to anger, to tears. I remember getting the proofs afterward. The first showed him serenely content, smiling at the camera. In the second, he was laughing delightedly as the photographer waved a stuffed animal in his face. In the next, he was beginning to get bored and had put on a cute little pout. The fourth showed him downright angry, with a defiant "just try to make me smile" look on his face. By the last shot, he had dissolved into tears. The poor little guy had had enough. Which of these pictures captured my son's personality? The answer, of course, is all of them! Each one caught a different side of his multifaceted nature. Together they give us an insightful glimpse into who he is.

This little story is a good analogy for the New Testament Gospels. Each of the four Gospels—Matthew, Mark, Luke, and John—paints a unique portrait of Jesus. Each provides special insight into who he is and what he accomplished. What are these four unique portraits? At the risk of oversimplifying, we may say that Matthew presents Jesus as the *Jewish Messiah*, the fulfillment of Old Testament hopes; Mark portrays him as the *suffering Son of God*, who offers himself as a sacrifice for sins; Luke's Jesus is the *Savior for all people*, who brings salvation to all nations and people groups; and in John, Jesus is the *eternal Son of God*, the self-revelation of God the Father. These are not contradictory portraits but complementary ones. Having four Gospels gives us a deeper, more profound understanding of Christology—the nature of Jesus' person and work.

There are also degrees of diversity among the Gospels. The first three—Matthew, Mark, and Luke—are known as the *Synoptic Gospels* (from the Greek *synopsis*, meaning "viewed together") because they view the life and ministry of Jesus from a similar perspective, follow the same general outline, and record a great deal of common material. The Gospel of John presents a very different perspective. The author of the fourth Gospel omits much material found in the Synoptics and includes much unique material. John also writes with a different style and dwells more on the theological significance of Jesus' words and deeds. We will discuss the uniqueness of John in greater detail in chapters 10 and 11.

THE GOSPEL GENRE

The first question readers must ask when approaching any literature is, "What am I reading?" This is the question of *genre*, or type of literature. If I pick up a newspaper and read, "The President Prepares to Address Congress," I recognize this as a news report and expect to read factual information. On the other hand, if I pick up a book and read, "Once upon a time, there were three bears," I know I am reading a fairy tale. I am not concerned about whether these bears actually existed, what country they were from, or whether they were grizzlies or brown bears. I read to be entertained and, perhaps, to look for moral lessons. In cases like these, we identify genre easily. But identification is not always so easy, and it is possible to misidentify literary genres. One person standing in a grocery store checkout line may read the *National Enquirer* headline "Aliens Invade Los Angeles" and fear that they are in mortal danger. Another identifies the genre as entertainment tabloid and chuckles. Identifying genre is essential for both interpretation and application.

To understand the Gospels, we must first ask, What kind of documents are these, and what sort of information are they meant to convey? Are they historical accounts meant to pass on factual information, or are they theological documents meant to teach spiritual truths? Or are they both? The identification of genre enables us to answer these questions. The genre of the Gospels may be examined under three headings: *history, narrative,* and *theology.*

The Gospels as History. The Gospels are historical in at least three ways. First, *they have a history of composition.* The Gospels did not fall from the sky. Stories about Jesus were passed down by his followers through word of mouth and then through written sources. The Gospel writers drew from these oral and written sources to compile their works. Appendix 1 discusses this process of transmission and various methods (*source, form,* and *redaction criticism*) that have been developed to study it.

Second, the Gospels are historical in that *they are set in a specific historical context.* This setting is first-century Palestine during the period of Roman occupation. To understand the Gospels, we must enter into the world in which they were written, a world very different from our own. In chapters 2 and 3, we will examine the historical and religious settings of the Gospels.

Third, the Gospels are historical in that *they are meant to convey accurate historical information.* This is implicit in all four Gospels and is explicitly stated by John (21:24) and especially by Luke (1:1–4). Luke leaves no doubt that he intends to write accurate history, claiming he received his information from eyewitnesses, that he "carefully investigated everything," and that he is writing so that Theophilus might know the "certainty" of the things he has been taught.

The historical nature of the Gospels has important implications for Christianity as a religion. The faith of the Gospel writers is based not on the esoteric teachings of a first-century philosopher nor on religious myths with symbolic meaning. It is based on the historical person and work of Jesus Christ. The Gospels claim to be the record of God's actions in human history through the person of his Son.

As an essentially historical religion, Christianity rises or falls on the historicity of core Gospel events: (1) Jesus' words and deeds, (2) his death on the cross, and (3) his resurrection, the vindication of his claims. As the apostle Paul writes with reference to Jesus' resurrection, "If Christ has not been raised, our preaching is useless and so is your faith" (1 Cor. 15:14). For Paul, as for the Gospel writers, the historicity of these events confirms the truth of Christianity. In chapter 12 we will examine some of the evidence for the historical reliability of the Gospels, and chapters 13–19 deal with questions related to the historical Jesus.

The Gospels as Narrative. While historical in nature, the Gospels are not merely collections of historical facts about Jesus. A second important feature of the Gospel genre is that these works are narratives, or stories. While all four Gospels concern the same basic historical events—the life, death, and resurrection of Jesus Christ—they present different perspectives on these events. They view characters from different angles. They develop plot in different ways. They emphasize different settings. Viewing the Gospels as story provides important insights into their literary and theological distinctions. Appendix 2 provides an in-depth discussion of narrative features and how these relate to the Gospels.

The Gospels as Theology. While the Gospels are meant to be historical, they are more than unbiased news reports. They are theological documents written to instruct and encourage believers and to convince unbelievers of the truth of their message. This is evident in that they focus especially on the saving work accomplished through the life, death, and resurrection of Jesus Christ. This is why we call the Gospel writers Evangelists (from *euangelizō*, "to announce good news"). They are proclaimers of the good news about Jesus Christ and the kingdom of God. Notice John's statement of intent in John 20:30–31: "Jesus performed many other signs in the presence of his disciples, which are not recorded in this book. But these are written that you may believe that Jesus is the Messiah, the Son of God, and that by believing you may have life in his name."

The recognition that the Gospel writers are theologians in their own right is one of the most important contributions of recent studies in the Gospels. Each Evangelist has a story to tell and a perspective to emphasize. Each brings out certain aspects of Jesus' identity. Notice the unique way each begins their work:

Matt. 1:1	This is the genealogy of Jesus the Messiah the son of David, the son of Abraham:
Mark 1:1	The beginning of the good news about Jesus the Messiah, the Son of God.

| Luke 1:1–4 | . . . since I myself have carefully investigated everything from the beginning, I too decided to write an orderly account . . . |
| John 1:1 | In the beginning was the Word, and the Word was with God, and the Word was God. |

Matthew begins with Jesus' Jewish ancestry, especially his descent through Abraham and David. This points forward to his focus on Jesus' fulfillment of the promises made to Israel. Mark introduces his story as a written account of the "good news" about Jesus and highlights Jesus' identity as Messiah and Son of God, two important titles in his work. Luke emphasizes his careful research and use of eyewitness testimony, confirming the historical reliability of his account. John introduces Jesus as the pre-existent Word of God, setting the stage for a Gospel centered on Jesus as the self-revelation of God. Although all four Gospels tell the story of Jesus, they approach it from different angles and with different emphases.

The identification of the Gospel writers as theologians has important implications for the way we read the Gospels. Each writer has a particular portrait of Jesus. Each has theological themes to develop. We ought to read each Gospel seeking to discern these theological themes.

In summary, we can classify the Gospels as *historical narrative motivated by theological concerns.* Their intention is not only to convey accurate historical material about Jesus but also to explain and interpret these salvation-bringing events. The Gospels were written not by detached, uninterested observers but by *Evangelists*, "proclaimers of good news," announcing the good news of Jesus the Messiah and calling people to faith in him.

WHY *FOUR* GOSPELS?

Each of the four Gospels was written to provide a unique perspective on the person and work of Jesus. Each also likely arose in a different community within the early church. But why did the church retain all four? The most famous early attempt to synthesize the four

Gospels into one was the *Diatessaron* ("through four"), compiled by the church father Tatian around AD 170. Tatian brought portions of all four Gospels together into one story. Since then, there have been many attempts to produce a "harmony" of the Gospels or to synthesize the Gospels into a single story. Yet in the end, the church has chosen to preserve the four distinct Gospels, recognizing each as a unique literary and theological masterpiece and as an inspired and authoritative work of the Holy Spirit.

READING "VERTICALLY": FOLLOWING THE STORYLINE

The nature of the Gospels as history, narrative, and theology teaches us much about how we ought to read them. If each Gospel writer has a unique perspective on the life of Jesus, and if the Holy Spirit inspired four Gospels instead of one, then we should respect the integrity of each story. It is important to read each Gospel on its own terms, following the progress of each narrative from introduction, to conflict, to climax, to resolution. Reading this way has been called *reading vertically*, following the story from top to bottom, from beginning to end. The alternative to such a vertical reading is a harmonistic approach, which brings the four Gospels together as one story. The danger of a harmony is that it risks obscuring and even distorting each Gospel's inspired and unique presentation.

We may illustrate this with an example. The four Gospels record seven sayings of Jesus from the cross. Many sermons have been preached on these seven last "words" of Jesus. While insight can be gained from this approach, the danger is that we will miss each writer's unique contribution. No Gospel records more than three of these sayings, and each has its own perspective on the crucifixion. In Mark, Jesus says only one thing from the cross: "My God, my God, why have you forsaken me?" The crucifixion is a dark and foreboding scene. The narrator intentionally draws the reader into Jesus' experience of isolation and despair. Introducing Luke's reassuring "Father, into your hands I commit my spirit" or John's triumphant "It is finished" misses Mark's point. Each Gospel has a story to tell. By reading vertically, we hear that story on its own terms.

READING "HORIZONTALLY": COMPARING THEIR ACCOUNTS

While there is a danger in harmonistically reading one Gospel's presentation into another, there can be benefits in comparing their accounts using a "synopsis," which places the Gospels in parallel columns. By comparing the Gospels to each other, we can identify each writer's distinct themes and theology. Comparing Luke with Matthew and Mark, we see that Luke often introduces statements about Jesus' prayer life, revealing his interest in Jesus' intimacy with the Father. We may call this *reading horizontally*—comparing the Gospels to discern each Evangelist's unique theological perspective. Reading horizontally is different from reading harmonistically. The latter risks missing each Evangelist's Spirit-inspired message by bringing the Gospels together as a single story. The former compares and contrasts them to discern each Gospel's unique themes and theology.

While reading the Gospels harmonistically risks missing each Gospel's unique message, a harmony can be beneficial when asking historical questions. The Gospels claim to be historical narratives, and so it is legitimate to investigate them from the perspective of what actually happened. Jesus' trial scene, for example, takes on different contours in each of the four Gospels. While a narrative theologian would ask about the themes of each Gospel writer, the historian asks basic historical questions: What role did the Jewish and Roman authorities play in the arrest of Jesus? Before whom was he tried? What accusations were made against him? Why was he crucified? The historian's task is to sift through all the available evidence to piece together a credible historical account. Here a harmonistic study could be helpful to glean as much information as possible from the available sources.

OTHER "GOSPELS"?

There are more than four ancient documents that claim to be gospels, or that contain stories about Jesus, including works like the *Gospel of Thomas*, the *Gospel of Peter*, and a number of infancy gospels, fanciful accounts of Jesus' birth and childhood. Browsing in a bookstore, you may come across books with sensationalistic titles like *The Unknown Gospels* or *The Lost Books of the Bible*. These so-called apocryphal gospels are neither lost nor unknown but are later writings about Jesus that the church rejected as inauthentic or otherwise unworthy to be included in Scripture.

While some scholars claim that these works may contain an occasional authentic tradition about Jesus, they are almost universally recognized as unreliable late compositions, pseudepigraphic (written under an assumed name), and dependent on the canonical Gospels. The sensational claim—made in books like *The DaVinci Code*—that these apocryphal gospels depict the "real Jesus" but were suppressed and silenced by the orthodox church, does not hold up under critical scrutiny. Though some Christians read and admired these writings, in the end, the church rejected them because they failed the test of historical authenticity and because they lacked the spiritual power and authority that indicated the inspiration by the Holy Spirit.

CONCLUSION

In this chapter we have identified the four canonical Gospels—Matthew, Mark, Luke, and John—as a unique blend of history, narrative, and theology. They are historical in that their purpose is to pass on accurate and reliable information about Jesus. They are narrative in that each has a unique story to tell, with its own development of plot, characters, and settings. They are theological in that the authors are passionate in their belief that Jesus is the Messiah and Savior of the world and their desire is to proclaim this good news to the ends of the earth. Though the Gospels were written at a specific time, in a specific place, and with specific purposes, they are of timeless benefit for the church.

Questions for Review and Discussion

1. What is a Gospel? Describe the Gospel genre.
2. Why do we have four Gospels instead of one? Should there be just one?
3. What might we miss if we harmonize the Gospels into a single story?

4. What does it mean to read the Gospels vertically?
5. What does it mean to read the Gospels horizontally?

Recommended Resources

Blomberg, Craig L. *Jesus and the Gospels*. 2nd ed. Nashville: B&H Academic, 2009.

Burridge, Richard A. *What Are the Gospels? A Comparison with Graeco-Roman Biography*. 2nd ed. Cambridge: Cambridge Univ. Press, 2004.

Strauss, Mark L. *Four Portraits, One Jesus: A Survey of Jesus and the Gospels*. Grand Rapids: Zondervan, 2007.

CHAPTER 2

THE HISTORICAL SETTING OF THE GOSPELS

At the end of the Old Testament period, the dominant power in the ancient Near East was the Medo-Persian Empire. Cyrus the Great conquered the Babylonian Empire in 539 BC and allowed the Jews to return to their land from exile and to rebuild Jerusalem and the temple (see the Old Testament books of Ezra and Nehemiah). When the reader opens the New Testament, four hundred years have passed, and the Roman Empire is now in control of the whole Mediterranean region. A summary of the historical events that took place during this four-century period is important for understanding the world in which Jesus lived and the nature of his ministry.

THE GREEK PERIOD (334–166 BC)

One of the most remarkable leaders of the ancient world was Alexander the Great (356–323 BC), who came to power after his father, Philip II, king of Macedon, was assassinated in 336 BC. Though only twenty years old, Alexander quickly consolidated his power in Greece and swept eastward with his army. He repeatedly defeated the Persians and, in a very short time, conquered the whole eastern Mediterranean, including Syria, Egypt, Persia, and Babylon. His empire reached as far as India.

While Alexander's swift conquest proved his military genius, his most influential role in history was his promotion of "Hellenization," which refers to the spread of Greek language and culture. Alexander had a great love for all things Greek and sought to introduce Greek ways throughout the territories he conquered. Although the Romans would later conquer the Greeks, in many ways the Greeks conquered the Romans, since the Romans adopted Greek models of art, literature, philosophy, and religion.

One of the most important results of Hellenization for the background to the New Testament was the emergence of *koine* ("common") Greek as the trade and diplomatic language of the eastern Mediterranean. Greek was viewed as the language of civilization, and anyone who did not speak Greek was considered a barbarian. The Israel of Jesus' day was trilingual. Hebrew was still used in religious contexts; Aramaic was the language of the common people; and Greek was the language of trade and government. (Latin would have also been spoken by Roman officials.) Jesus probably conversed in all three languages, though most of his teaching was in Aramaic. The New Testament books and letters are all written in Greek.

When Alexander died suddenly in 323 BC (at only thirty-three years old!), a power struggle ensued for control of his empire. War and conflict between his four leading generals eventually resulted in the establishment of two great dynasties. The dynasty of the Ptolemies was centered in Egypt, with Alexandria as its capital. The dynasty of the Seleucids was centered in Syria, with Antioch as its capital. Because Israel was strategically located between Syria and Egypt, it became caught in a tug-of-war between these two rivals. The Ptolemies gained control of Israel and ruled her for 125 years. The Jews lived in relative peace and prosperity under Ptolemaic rule. One of the most significant literary achievements of this period was the translation of the *Septuagint* (abbreviated LXX), the Greek translation of the Old Testament. The Septuagint became the primary Bible of Jews scattered throughout the Mediterranean world. The Septuagint was also extremely important for the spread of Christianity, since it provided the early Christians with a Bible that was understandable to both Jews and Gentiles.

There was constant war and strife between the Ptolemies of Egypt and the Seleucids of Syria. The Seleucids finally gained control of Judea in 198 BC under the king Antiochus III. When Antiochus's son, Antiochus IV, came to the throne in 175 BC, the Jews faced one of their greatest crises ever. Antiochus pushed hard to bring Israel fully into his empire by turning it into a Hellenistic state. He increased taxation and repeatedly looted the treasures of the Jerusalem temple.

He sold the office of Jewish high priest to the highest bidder. He encouraged pagan altars and the building of a Greek gymnasium in the holy city of Jerusalem. Many Jews became fascinated by Hellenism and so were receptive to such changes, but others were outraged. Increasing division arose in Israel between *Hellenists*, Jews who favored the adoption of Greek ideas, and conservative *Hasidim* (meaning "holy ones"), who opposed them.

Antiochus referred to himself as "Epiphanes," meaning "divine one" or "god manifest," but his opponents nicknamed him "Epimanes," meaning "madman"! Over time, he moved to destroy Judaism. Sabbath observance, circumcision, and keeping the law were banned. Copies of Scripture were confiscated and burned. An altar dedicated to Zeus was set up in the Jerusalem temple, and pigs and other unclean animals were offered as sacrifices. This desecration of the temple is referred to in the book of Daniel as the "abomination that causes desolation" (Dan. 11:31; 12:11). Jesus would later draw on this powerful imagery to predict the horrors of the siege and destruction of Jerusalem in AD 70 (Mark 13:14 par.).

THE MACCABEES AND JEWISH INDEPENDENCE (166–63 BC)

Though the desecration of the temple by Antiochus Epiphanes was one of the darkest times in Jewish history, it gave way to one of the brightest. Rebellion against the Seleucids broke out in the Judean village of Modein when an old priest named Mattathias killed a Syrian official who had ordered him to offer a pagan sacrifice. Mattathias fled with his five sons into the hills, where they launched a guerrilla war against the Syrians. The rebellion became known as the *Maccabean Revolt*, named after Mattathias's son Judas "Maccabeus." Maccabeus means "hammer" and was a nickname given to Judas because of his reputation as a warrior.

On Chislev (December) 25, 164 BC, exactly three years after the desecration of the temple by Antiochus Epiphanes, Judas recaptured Jerusalem and reinitiated Jewish sacrifices. This victory became commemorated in the Jewish festival of *Hanukkah*, meaning "dedication" (also called the Festival of Lights).

After Judas was killed in battle in 160 BC, leadership passed to his brothers, first Jonathan (160–143 BC) and then Simon (143–135 BC). Simon eventually gained full political independence from the Syrians, taking the title of leader and high priest. He thus established the *Hasmonean dynasty* (named after Hasmon, an ancestor of Mattathias), a line of priest-kings who would rule Israel for one hundred years, until the Roman occupation in 63 BC.

THE ROMAN PERIOD (63 BC–AD 135)

Roman domination of Israel began in 63 BC, when the Roman general Pompey captured a Jerusalem weakened by civil war between two Hasmoneans, Hyrcanus II and Aristobulus II. The conquering Romans made Hyrcanus II high priest and ruler of the Jews. The real power behind the throne, however, lay with Hyrcanus's chief advisor, a man named Antipater who had gained the favor of the Romans. The Romans made Antipater governor of Judea, and he appointed his sons Phasael and Herod as military governors of Jerusalem and Galilee. Although Antipater was an *Idumean* (or Edomite) rather than a Jew, the Romans made little distinction since the Jews had ruled Idumea under the Hasmoneans.

When Antipater was killed in 43 BC, a power struggle ensued between Antigonus, the son of Aristobolus II, and Antipater's two sons, Herod and Phasael. Phasael was captured and committed suicide, but Herod fled to Rome. There he appealed to the Romans for help and was appointed king of Judea. Returning to Israel with a Roman army, he defeated and executed Antigonus, the last of the Hasmonean rulers. The Hasmonean dynasty was over, and the Herodian dynasty had begun.

Herod "the Great" ruled as king of the Jews under Roman authority for thirty-three years, from 37–4 BC. It is this Herod who appears in the account of Jesus' birth (Matt. 2:1–19; Luke 1:5). Herod was a strange mix of an efficient ruler and a cruel tyrant. On the one hand, he was distrustful, jealous, and brutal, ruthlessly crushing any potential opposition. Because he was an Idumean, the Jews never accepted him as their legitimate king. Having usurped the Hasmonean rulers, he constantly feared conspiracy. To legitimize his claim to the throne, he married a Hasmonean princess named Miriamne, later murdering her when he suspected she was plotting against him. Three of his sons, another wife, and his mother-in-law met the same fate when they were suspected of conspiracy. The Roman emperor Augustus once said he would rather be Herod's pig *(hus)* than his son *(huios)*, a play on words in Greek. Herod, trying to be a legitimate Jew, would not eat pork, but he freely murdered his sons! Matthew's account of Herod's slaughter of the infants in Bethlehem (Matt. 2:1–18) fits well with what we know of the king's ambition, paranoia, and cruelty.

At the same time, Herod was an extremely efficient ruler. He was a loyal subject to the Roman emperor, Caesar Augustus, maintaining order in Israel and protecting the eastern flank of the Roman Empire. He also viewed himself as a great protector of Judaism. He encouraged the development of the synagogue communities and in time of calamity canceled taxes and supplied the people with free grain. He was also a great builder, a role that earned him the title "the Great." His greatest project was the rebuilding and beautification of the temple in Jerusalem, restoring it to even greater splendor than in the time of Solomon.

Herod died in 4 BC (cf. Matt. 2:19), probably from intestinal cancer. As a final act of vengeance against his rebellious subjects, he rounded up leading Jews and commanded that at his death they should be executed. His reasoning was that if there was no mourning *for* his death, at least there would be mourning *at* his death! At Herod's death, the order was overruled and the prisoners were released.

THE HERODIAN DYNASTY

After Herod's death, his kingdom was divided among three of his sons. Archelaus was appointed ruler of Judea, Samaria, and Idumea (see Matt. 2:21–23). Archelaus ruled poorly, however, and the emperor removed him from office in AD 6. Judea and Samaria were transferred to the control of Roman governors. The most important of these for the study of the Gospels is Pontius Pilate (governor of Judea from AD 26 to 36), under whose administration Jesus was crucified.

A second son of Herod the Great, Herod Antipas, became ruler of Galilee and Perea. This is the Herod of Jesus' public ministry. He imprisoned and eventually executed John the Baptist (Luke 3:19–20; Mark 6:17–29). He also wondered about Jesus' identity when people speculated that John had risen from the dead (Mark 6:14–16 par.).

Eventually, Antipas got his wish to see Jesus, when Pilate sent Jesus to stand before him at his trial (Luke 23:7–12; cf. Acts 4:27).

A third son, Herod Philip, became tetrarch of Iturea, Trachonitis, Gaulanitis, Auranitis, and Batanea, regions north and east of Galilee. He is mentioned in the New Testament only in Luke 3:1 (the Philip of Mark 6:17 is a different son of Herod the Great).

ROMAN RULE AND THE *PAX ROMANA*

When Caesar Augustus became emperor in 31 BC, the Roman Empire entered a period of relative peace known as the *Pax Romana* ("Roman Peace"). Never before had the whole Mediterranean region had the kind of political stability that Rome brought. The Mediterranean Sea became a "Roman lake."

The stability brought by Roman occupation allowed relative freedom of travel and a large degree of order throughout the empire, a situation ideal for the spread of Christianity. The Romans built roads for their armies, which greatly aided travelers, including early Christian missionaries. The Roman system of law and order gave Christians a measure of protection as they went from town to town preaching the gospel.

The seat of Roman government in Judea was at Caesarea on the Mediterranean coast, but the governor would come to Jerusalem to maintain order during the various festivals. This is why Pontius Pilate was present in Jerusalem for Passover during Jesus' trial. While the Roman governors had a mixed history of tolerance and oppression, most exhibited a general insensitivity toward the Jews. There was frequent unrest and occasional outbreaks of revolt. The Romans responded to these with a ruthless violence, massacring anyone who would challenge Roman authority.

The cost of maintaining the vast Roman Empire was enormous, and Rome imposed a variety of taxes on its citizens. Direct taxes were collected by officials of the emperor, but the right to collect indirect taxes was generally leased to the highest bidder. This system was open to great abuse, since Rome did not generally control the surcharges imposed by their agents. Tax collectors were despised by the common people, not just because of their reputation for extortion but also because they worked for the hated Romans.

THE JEWISH REVOLT OF AD 66–73

Various factors made Palestine a hotbed of rebellion and political unrest:

1. Traditional conflict between Hellenizers and conservatives
2. Widespread oppression by wealthy aristocrats and landowners
3. Severe Roman taxation
4. Heavy-handed Roman suppression of opposition
5. At times incompetent and insensitive Roman administration

These factors, together with the history of successful revolt under the Maccabees, set the stage for the Jewish Revolt of AD 66–73.

Various protests and minor revolts had occurred throughout the first century, but all had been quickly suppressed by the Romans. Full-scale rebellion erupted in AD 66. The emperor Nero sent his general Vespasian to put down the revolt. Vespasian began conquering the cities of Galilee and Judea, but the siege of Jerusalem was delayed when Nero died and a struggle ensued over his succession. Vespasian was proclaimed emperor by his troops and returned to Rome to defeat his rivals, leaving his son Titus to complete the battle for Jerusalem. In AD 70, after a horrific siege, Jerusalem was taken and the temple destroyed. The Jewish historian Josephus, who was present during the siege, portrays it in gruesome detail. Many died from a terrible famine; others were killed by Jewish infighting; many thousands more were slaughtered when the Romans breached the walls.

Though pockets of Jewish resistance held out for several years after Jerusalem's collapse, defeat was inevitable. The last citadel to fall was the mountaintop fortress at Masada in AD 73. To reach it, the Romans built a massive earthen ramp, which is still visible today. According to Josephus, when the Romans finally breached the walls, they found that the nine hundred Jewish defenders had committed suicide rather than surrender.

The early church historian Eusebius claims that prior to the destruction of Jerusalem, the Jewish Christians there received an oracle telling them to flee the city and go to the town of Pella in the Decapolis. In this way, many escaped the destruction.

AFTER THE WAR

The war had a profound and transforming effect on Judaism. With the destruction of the temple, the Sadducees and the priestly leadership lost their influence and eventually disappeared from history. Study of Torah (the law of Moses) and worship in the synagogue replaced the sacrificial system as the heart of Jewish religious life.

The destruction of Jerusalem also had a major impact on the young Christian movement. Jesus had predicted the destruction of Jerusalem, and Christians saw her collapse and the cessation of the temple ritual and sacrifices as God's judgment on Israel for rejecting the Messiah and as divine vindication that a new era of salvation had begun. This new era was based not on animal sacrifices but on Jesus' once-for-all sacrifice on the cross. The geographic and ethnic center of Christianity also shifted after the war. While before, Christians saw Jerusalem as the mother church, afterward Jewish Christianity decreased in influence. The split with Judaism that had begun throughout the Christian communities gained momentum.

Questions for Review and Discussion

1. Summarize (briefly) the main events of the history of Israel from the close of the Old Testament to the destruction of Jerusalem in AD 70.
2. What sparked the Maccabean revolt? What was its result?
3. Who was Herod the Great? Who was Herod Antipas?
4. Describe the significance of Roman rule for the Israel of Jesus' day.

Recommended Resources

Bruce, F. F. *New Testament History.* Garden City, NY: Doubleday, 1980.

Cohen, S. J. D. *From the Maccabees to the Mishnah.* 3rd ed. Philadelphia: Westminster John Knox, 2014.

Ferguson, E. *Backgrounds of Early Christianity.* 3rd ed. Grand Rapids: Eerdmans, 2003.

CHAPTER 3

THE RELIGIOUS SETTING OF THE GOSPELS: FIRST-CENTURY JUDAISM

The Judaism of Jesus' day was not a single, unified religion. Rather it was a relatively diverse collection of movements and belief systems. Some scholars even speak of the Judaisms (plural) of the first century. Before discussing this diversity, we will identify certain core beliefs that all Jews shared.

CORE JEWISH BELIEFS

Monotheism. Fundamental to Judaism was belief in the one true God, Yahweh, who created the heavens and the earth. All other gods were mere idols, unworthy of worship. This belief distinguished Judaism from all the polytheistic religions of the Greco-Roman world.

The Covenant. The one true God had entered into a covenant relationship with the people of Israel. The covenant was originally given to Abraham, who was promised God's blessings, a great nation, and a land for his descendants (Gen. 12:1–3; 15:1–21). The Abrahamic covenant was applied to the nation of Israel in the Mosaic covenant, given to Israel through Moses at Mount Sinai (Exodus 19–20).

The Law (Torah): Standards for Covenant Faithfulness. Israel's responsibility in its covenant relationship was to remain faithful to God's law (Torah), the body of commandments given to Israel (Exodus 19, 24). Faithfulness to the law, and hence the covenant, would bring blessings and prosperity in the land of Israel. Unfaithfulness would mean judgment and exile. Especially important to the law were various identity markers: (1) *worship of Yahweh* alone, (2) *circumcision* for all male children, (3) observance of a weekly *Sabbath* rest, and (4) *dietary laws* prohibiting the eating of certain "unclean" or ceremonially defiled foods. When Judaism came into conflict with other cultures and religions, these were the fundamentals to which the Jews rallied.

The landscape of first-century Judaism may best be surveyed by distinguishing two important and parallel institutions: (1) the *Jerusalem temple* with its priesthood and sacrificial system, and (2) the *local synagogues* centered on the study of Torah.

TEMPLE, PRIESTHOOD, AND SACRIFICES

The Jerusalem temple was the center of Israel's religious life. The book of Deuteronomy identifies this central sanctuary as the only place where sacrifices may be made (Deut. 12:5–14)—the one temple for the one God. Before the temple, Israel had a portable tabernacle, which they carried around with them in the wilderness after the exodus from Egypt (Exodus 25–30). The first Jerusalem temple was built by King Solomon but was subsequently destroyed by the Babylonians in 587 BC. The second Jerusalem temple, built by Zerubbabel after the exile, was greatly expanded by Herod the Great and transformed into one of the most magnificent buildings of the ancient world (cf. Mark 13:1).

The design of the temple was meant to reflect the holiness of God, with a series of concentric courtyards moving toward greater exclusivity. Non-Jews could go no farther than the outer Court of the Gentiles, where signs warned of death for any who transgressed. Moving inward, one came to the Court of Women (for all Israelites), the Court of Israel (for ritually pure males), and finally the Court of Priests, where the temple building proper stood. In this courtyard, priests offered daily burnt sacrifices. The temple building itself was divided into two chambers, each protected by a large curtain. The first, the Holy Place, would be entered by a priest only twice a day to burn incense. The inner Holy of Holies, the most sacred place in Judaism, was entered only once a year by the high priest on the Day of Atonement.

The temple compound was more than a place of sacrifices. It was also a center for judicial, religious, and community life. Worship was conducted here, with choirs of Levites singing, prayers being offered (Luke 18:10–11; 24:53), tithes being collected (Mark 12:41), and festivals being celebrated. Rabbis taught here (Mark 14:49), and the Sanhedrin—the Jewish high court—held its sessions.

The *Levites* were descendants of Levi, one of the twelve sons of Jacob. Unlike the other tribes of Israel, they were not given a tribal inheritance in the land but rather were consecrated as God's special tribe in place of the firstborn of all the Israelites (Num. 3:41, 45; 8:18; 35:2–3; Deut. 18:1; Josh. 14:3). The *priests* were also Levites but were more specifically descendants of Aaron, the brother of Moses and first high priest of Israel (Ex. 28:1–3). The functions of the priests were to offer daily sacrifices, maintain the temple grounds, collect tithes, pronounce blessings, and perform purification rites (Leviticus 13–14; cf. Mark 1:44).

The priests were overseen by the *high priest*, who held the highest religious office in Judaism. The office was hereditary and a lifelong appointment. The high priest had the once-a-year privilege of entering the Holy of Holies on the Day of Atonement to offer sacrifices for the entire nation (Lev. 16:1–34; Heb. 9:6–7). The high priest was also head of the *Sanhedrin*, the Jewish high court made up of seventy elders (*m. Sanh.* 1:6). Caiaphas was the high priest in Jesus' time (Matt. 26:3, 57; John 11:49), though his father-in-law, Annas, who had been deposed earlier by the Romans, also exercised a great deal of influence (Luke 3:2; John 18:13–14, 24; Acts 4:6). The Gospels also speak of high priests in the plural (usually translated "chief priests"). These were probably the wealthy aristocratic priests of Jerusalem.

The power of the priesthood waxed and waned depending on the political situation. It reached its zenith under the later Hasmoneans, who took on the authority of both high priest and king. It diminished greatly under Herod the Great, who reserved the right to appoint the high priest. During the period of Roman governors, the high priest and the Sanhedrin regained a powerful role.

SYNAGOGUES, SCRIBES, AND THE STUDY OF TORAH

While the temple in Jerusalem was the center of Jewish worship, Judaism was becoming more decentralized with the growth in synagogue communities throughout the Roman Empire. Synagogues were Jewish meeting places for worship, education, and community gatherings. The origin of the synagogue is uncertain but probably goes back to the Babylonian exile, after the temple of Solomon was destroyed. During the Second Temple period, the synagogue and the temple both functioned as key institutions for Jewish worship. Wherever ten Jewish males lived, a synagogue could be formed.

One of the most important developments in the postexilic Jewish communities was the establishment of the profession of *scribe*. Also called "teachers of the law," "lawyers," and "rabbis" in the New Testament, scribes were experts in the interpretation and teaching of the law of Moses. As the teaching of Torah gained a more central place in the life of Judaism, the scribal office took on greater importance and influence.

Unlike the priesthood, the scribal office was gained not through inheritance but through knowledge and ability. A group of students would gather around a teacher, seeking entrance into his "school." Those with promise would be examined and, if accepted, would accompany him, watching his lifestyle and learning from him. According to Acts 22:3, Paul was educated at the feet of Gamaliel, one of the leading rabbis of Jerusalem.

Most New Testament references to scribes are negative, and scribes are condemned together with the Pharisees for their legalism and hypocrisy. Jesus' dynamic teaching and personal authority are set in contrast to the behavior of the scribes, who merely recited the traditions of the past (Mark 1:22). Yet Jesus speaks of the validity of the position in Matthew 13:52: "Every teacher of the law who has become a disciple in the kingdom of heaven is like the owner of a house who brings out of his storeroom new treasures as well as old" (cf. Matt. 23:1–2).

GROUPS WITHIN JUDAISM

Sadducees. The origin of the Sadducees is uncertain, but they appear to have arisen from the priestly families of the Jerusalem aristocracy who supported the Hasmonean dynasty. In Jesus' day, the Sadducees controlled the priesthood and most political affairs, dominating the

Sanhedrin (Acts 5:17). Because of their political involvement, they were more open to Hellenistic influence than were the Pharisees or Essenes (see the following).

The Sadducees considered only the Pentateuch, the first five books of Moses, to be fully authoritative Scripture, denying the oral traditions of the Pharisees. The Sadducees also differed from the Pharisees by rejecting belief in predestination (or determinism), the immortality of the soul, and the resurrection of the body (Acts 23:8).

Since the Sadducean power base was the priesthood and the temple, the destruction of Jerusalem in AD 70 ended their political influence, and the group disappeared from history.

Pharisees. The Pharisees probably arose from the Hasidim, the pious Jews who had fought with the Maccabees against the oppression of Antiochus Epiphanes (see previous chapter). They then split off in opposition to the Hellenizing tendency of the later Hasmoneans. Josephus claims they numbered about six thousand. While the Sadducees were mostly upper-class aristocrats and priests, the Pharisees appear to have been primarily middle-class laypeople, perhaps craftsmen and merchants. The Sadducees had greater political power, but the Pharisees had broader support among the people.

The most distinctive characteristic of the Pharisees was their strict adherence to Torah, not only the written law but also the oral law, a body of traditions (the "tradition of the elders" [Mark 7:3]) which expanded and elaborated on the Old Testament law. The term *Pharisee* is probably derived from a Hebrew word for "separatists" *(perushim)* and was applied because of the dietary and purity laws that restricted table fellowship with the common people and with non-Jews.

In contrast to the Sadducees, the Pharisees believed in the resurrection of the dead (Acts 23:8) and steered a middle road between the Sadducees' belief in free will and the predestination (determinism) of the Essenes. They also cultivated a strong hope in the coming of the Messiah, the Son of David, who would deliver them from foreign oppression.

According to the Gospels, Jesus came into frequent conflict with the Pharisees. He condemned them for raising their traditions to the level of Scripture and for focusing on the outward requirements of the law while ignoring matters of the heart (Luke 11:39–44; Matt.

23:23–26). For their part, the separatist Pharisees attacked Jesus' association with tax collectors and sinners (Mark 2:13–17 par.; Luke 15:1–2; etc.) and the way he placed himself above Sabbath regulations (Mark 2:23–28 par.). Despite these differences, Jesus was much closer theologically to the Pharisees than to the Sadducees, sharing belief in the authority of Scripture, the resurrection, and the coming of the Messiah. His frequent conflicts arose because he challenged the Pharisees on their own turf and because they viewed him as a threat to their leadership and influence over the people.

After the destruction of the temple and its sacrificial system, Judaism was renewed as a religion centered on the study of Torah. This became known as *rabbinic Judaism*. There is a relatively unbroken line of tradition from the teachings of Pharisaic Judaism, to rabbinic Judaism, to modern Orthodox Judaism.

Essenes. Like the Pharisees, the Essenes probably grew out of the Hasidim movement. They were similar to the Pharisees in their beliefs but were even more separatist. They rigorously kept the law, developing their own strict legal code. They refused to offer sacrifices in the Jerusalem temple because they regarded the temple as polluted by a corrupt priesthood. Some Essenes married and lived in villages throughout Israel, while others lived in celibacy in monastic settlements.

Most scholars believe that the *Qumran community* that produced the *Dead Sea Scrolls* were Essenes. According to what can be pieced together from the scrolls, this community began when a group of priests withdrew from the Jerusalem priesthood and moved to the Judean wilderness near the Dead Sea. This withdrawal resulted from opposition to the Hasmonean priest-kings, whom they viewed as illegitimate rulers. The Qumran sectarians were greatly influenced by a leader known as the Teacher of Righteousness, who was persecuted by a Jerusalem high priest identified in the scrolls as the Wicked Priest (perhaps John Hyrcanus, who ruled from 135 to 104 BC).

The Qumran group was "apocalyptic" in its perspective, meaning that they viewed themselves as the true Israel facing the imminent end of the age. They expected that God would soon intervene to deliver his people and that they would join God's angels in a great war against the Romans and Jewish apostates. The group expected not a single messiah but two: a military messiah from the line of

David and a priestly messiah from the line of Aaron. The Qumran community was presumably destroyed by the Romans in the Jewish Revolt of AD 66–73.

There are some interesting parallels between early Christianity and the Qumran sect. Both considered themselves God's righteous remnant, those few who had remained faithful to his covenant promises despite the apostasy of others (see Rom. 11:1–10). Both were eschatologically oriented, with expectations of an imminent end of the present age. Both interpreted the Old Testament with reference to events in their recent past and near future. Yet there were also important differences. The Qumran sectarians were very legalistic and exclusive and looked to the *future* coming of their messiahs. Christians, by contrast, claimed that with the coming of Jesus the Messiah, the end times had already begun. God's promises were now being fulfilled through Jesus' life, death, and resurrection and through the worldwide proclamation of the gospel. The salvation to be consummated in the future had already been achieved.

Zealots, Social Bandits, and Other Revolutionaries. As we have seen, first-century Israel was a hotbed of revolutionary activity. Some of this activity centered on *social banditry*, arising from the economic deprivation of the peasantry in Israel. Social bandits were the Robin Hoods of first-century Israel, attacking the elite and powerful upper class within Israel, and the Roman authorities who protected them. Other movements might be called *messianic*, in that they had political aims to overthrow the Roman rulers and establish an independent Jewish state. Still others were *prophetic*, centered on a charismatic leader who gained a popular following by claiming that God's deliverance was about to take place.

The Romans and their sympathizers considered all such movements to be made up of thugs and bandits engaged in terrorist activities. But most common people considered them freedom fighters, seeking to rid Israel of foreign oppression. Unable to defeat the Romans in open battle, the rebels engaged in guerrilla warfare, raiding Roman garrisons and attacking Jews who collaborated with the enemy. A number of figures involved in this kind of insurrection and social banditry are mentioned in the New Testament (Matt. 27:16; Mark 15:7, 27; Luke 23:19; John 18:40; cf. Acts 3:14; 5:36; 21:38).

One of Jesus' disciples, Simon, is identified as "the Zealot" (Mark 3:18 par.; Acts 1:13), but it is uncertain whether he was a former rebel or this is a description of his zeal for the law (see Acts 21:20; 22:3).

Herodians. Mentioned only three times in the Gospels (Mark 3:6; 12:13; Matt. 22:16), the Herodians may be viewed as the political opposites of social bandits and revolutionaries. They were supporters of the pro-Roman Herodian dynasty. During Jesus' ministry, they were based primarily in Galilee and Perea, where Herod Antipas ruled.

People of the Land. It should be noted that all of these groups made up only a small percentage of the Jewish population. Most people were not members of any group but were merely common "people of the land" (Hebrew: *Am-ha-Eretz*), poor farmers, craftsmen, and merchants. In general, they hated Roman rule and taxation and respected the piety of the Pharisees and the scribes. Most were eagerly awaiting a political messiah who would overthrow the harsh Roman rule (see Luke 3:15).

Questions for Review and Discussion

1. What core beliefs did most all Jews share?
2. Who were the Levites? The priests? The high priest? What was the Sanhedrin?
3. What were the background and beliefs of the Pharisees, the Sadducees, and the Essenes?

Recommended Resources

Charlesworth, James H., ed. *The Messiah: Developments in Earliest Judaism and Christianity.* Minneapolis: Fortress, 2009.

Nickelsburg, G. W. E. *Jewish Literature between the Bible and the Mishnah: A Historical and Literary Introduction.* Philadelphia: Fortress, 2011.

Sanders, E. P. *Judaism: Practice and Belief 63 BCE—66 CE.* Philadelphia: Fortress, 2016.

CHAPTER 4

INTRODUCING MATTHEW'S GOSPEL

I glanced out my window when I heard the bicycles pull up. Two young men in white shirts and ties were getting off their bikes, each carrying several books and pamphlets. I immediately recognized them as Mormons. I had mixed feelings. On the one hand, I groaned at the thought of stopping my work and losing precious time. On the other hand, I felt a measure of excitement at the opportunity to share my faith with two who held a very different perspective from my own. When they knocked on the door, I opened it and invited them in. I could tell they were a bit taken aback by my friendliness, and perhaps a little suspicious. Without thinking, I made the faux pas of offering them a Coke (Mormons avoid caffeine). We laughed and, the ice now broken, sat down for a discussion. Before long, the conversation turned to the nature of authentic faith. "But we are Christians!" one of my new friends insisted. "The Book of Mormon is really the completion of the Christian faith, God's final revelation through Joseph Smith." From there, the conversation turned to the truth or falsity of the claims of Joseph Smith. Is Mormonism in fact the completion of God's plan of salvation? Or is it a dangerous sect distorting the authentic message of the gospel?

In many ways, Matthew's Gospel is just such a discussion and debate. It is an extended defense, in narrative form, of the claim that a new sect within Judaism, known originally as "the Way" and later as Christianity, in fact is authentic Judaism, the completion or fulfillment of God's purpose for Israel and the world. At the time of its writing, the debate has reached a fevered pitch, with strong words flying in both directions. The authentic people of God, the narrator emphatically affirms, are defined no longer by ancestry or ethnic identity but by allegiance to Jesus the Messiah. The risen Lord is now calling forth disciples from all nations, Jews and Gentiles alike—a new people of God.

WHO WROTE MATTHEW'S GOSPEL?

Like the other three Gospels, Matthew's Gospel is, strictly speaking, anonymous. By this we mean the author is not named in the Gospel itself. The title "According to Matthew" *(kata Maththaion)* was probably added when the Gospels were brought together into a collection. Yet early church tradition unanimously ascribes the first Gospel to Matthew, a tax collector who became a disciple of Jesus. All three Synoptics list Matthew as one of Jesus' twelve disciples (Matt. 10:3; Mark 3:18; Luke 6:15; cf. Acts 1:13). The Gospel of Matthew explicitly identifies him as "the tax collector" (10:3) and narrates the story of his call by Jesus (9:9–13). Mark and Luke relate this same story but identify the tax collector as Levi (Mark 2:14–17; Luke 5:27–32), naming Matthew only in their lists of disciples. While some scholars claim that these were two separate individuals, it is more likely that Matthew and Levi are two names for the same person.

Some have claimed that evidence from the Gospel itself points to Matthew as the author: (1) the skillful organization of the Gospel (a tax collector would have organizational skills), (2) the use of the name Matthew in 9:9, and (3) the prominence of money and tax-collecting themes (10:3; 17:24–27; 18:23–25; 20:1–16; 27:3–5; 28:11–15). On its own, this evidence carries little weight, suggesting only that someone like Matthew wrote the Gospel. A counterargument is that the Gospel's emphasis on Jewish ritual and the law would not fit a tax collector, who would be an outsider to religious affairs. Some have suggested that the author was a converted scribe or Pharisee. They point to Matthew 13:52 as a possible self-designation: "Every teacher of the law who has become a disciple in the kingdom of heaven is like the owner of a house who brings out of his storeroom new treasures as well as old." Is Matthew this Jewish teacher, bringing his scholarly training in Jewish tradition (the old treasures) into the service of the kingdom of God (the new)?

The mixed data means a conclusion on authorship must be made with caution. In the absence of better evidence, the strong church tradition tips the scale in favor of Matthew's authorship. It seems unlikely that the early church would ascribe the work to a relatively obscure figure like Matthew unless they had good reason to do so. Uncertain authorship, of course, does not render questionable the authority or inspiration of the text. The authors of many Old Testament books and at least one New Testament book (Hebrews) are unknown.

WHY WAS MATTHEW'S GOSPEL WRITTEN?

Matthew has long been recognized as the "Jewish Gospel" because of its Jewish features and orientation. That the author is writing to a predominantly Jewish or a mixed Jewish and Gentile audience is suggested by the many Jewish terms and customs presented without explanation (ceremonial washings, 15:2; the temple tax, 17:24–27; phylacteries and tassels, 23:5; whitewashed tombs, 23:27). At the same time, the Gospel is written in Greek, so we are probably to think of a Greek-speaking Jewish environment (perhaps Syria—see the following).

The primary purpose of the Gospel is to demonstrate that Jesus is the fulfillment of Jewish hopes for the Messiah. The coming of the Messiah represents the climax of salvation history, the fulfillment of God's plan to bring salvation to his people Israel and to the Gentile nations.

It is likely that this theme has, at least in part, an *apologetic* goal, providing the church with a response against those who are denying that Jesus is the Messiah and that the church, made up of Jews and Gentiles, is the authentic people of God in the present age. The implication is that the author's community is in conflict and debate with the larger Jewish community. Notice, for example, the negative portrayal of the Jewish leaders (chap. 23, etc.), the culpability of the Jewish crowds at Jesus' trial (27:25), and Jewish reports "to this very day" that the disciples stole the body of Jesus (27:62–66; 28:11–15). In response to such accusations, the author seeks to show that the authentic people of God are those who have responded in faith to Jesus the Messiah.

A second narrative purpose is to call the church to greater faith and trust in their risen and ever-present Lord. This is suggested by Matthew's references to the still-future church (16:18; 18:17), his emphasis on the abiding presence of the risen Christ in the church (18:20; 28:20), and his frequent use of the exalted title "Lord" for Jesus.

WHEN AND WHERE WAS MATTHEW'S GOSPEL WRITTEN?

Though the Gospel does not indicate its place of origin, a significant number of scholars have proposed Antioch in Syria as a likely location. The earliest quotation from Matthew comes from Ignatius, bishop of Antioch, around AD 115. The Gospel also seems to have been used as a source for the *Didache*, a church manual probably produced in Syria around AD 100. The likelihood that the Gospel was written in Greek to Jewish Christians also fits Antioch, since the church was founded when Greek-speaking Jewish Christians fled there from Jerusalem (Acts 11:19–21). The debate over authentic Judaism and the author's concern for Gentiles is also appropriate to this location, since the city had large Jewish and Gentile populations, and since the church there was missions minded, sending Paul and Barnabas on their first missionary journey (Acts 13:1–2).

The date of Matthew is disputed. Some place the Gospel in the 80s or 90s, after the church has broken away from the Jewish synagogue. A later date may also be suggested in Matthew's parable of the wedding banquet, which speaks of the king who "sent his army and destroyed those murderers and burned their city" (Matt. 22:7). Some see here an allusion to the Roman destruction of Jerusalem in AD 70, interpreted as God's judgment for the crucifixion of Jesus.

Others favor an earlier date, in the 60s, claiming that there is no indication in 24:1–28 that the destruction of Jerusalem has already occurred. An early date is also suggested by church tradition. Irenaeus wrote around AD 175 that "Matthew also issued a written Gospel among the Hebrews in their own dialect while Peter and Paul were preaching at Rome and laying the foundations of the church" (Irenaeus, *Against Heresies* 3.1.1). Irenaeus's statement is suspect, however, since Matthew does not seem to have been originally written in Hebrew, and since neither Peter nor Paul founded the church in Rome (it was already long established when Paul wrote Romans around AD 55). A firm conclusion on the date of Matthew remains elusive.

LITERARY FEATURES OF MATTHEW'S GOSPEL

Among the four Gospels, Matthew shows the most evidence of careful structure and design. The author is clearly a skilled literary artist.

Concise Style. Whereas Mark has a lively, expansive style with lots of details, Matthew is generally shorter and more concise. For example, the account of the raising of Jairus's daughter takes 345 words in Greek in Mark, but only 139 words in Matthew. Mark writes more like a storyteller, Matthew more like a reporter.

Fulfillment Formulas and Old Testament Quotations. One of Matthew's most distinctive structural features is his use of "fulfillment formulas" to demonstrate that the events of Jesus' life fulfilled Old Testament prophecies. Ten times, the narrator uses a similar formula: *"This was to fulfill what was spoken by the prophet, saying . . ."* followed by an Old Testament quotation (1:22–23; 2:15; 2:17–18; 2:23; 4:14–16; 8:17; 12:17–21; 13:35; 21:4–5; 27:9–10). In many other passages, the Old Testament is identified as fulfilled in Jesus' words and deeds.

Topical Arrangement. While all of the Gospels at times utilize a topical rather than chronological arrangement, this is especially true of Matthew. There are collections of teaching (chaps. 5–7), miracle stories (chaps. 8–9), mission instructions (chap. 10), parables (chap. 13), teachings about the church (chap. 18), denunciations against the religious leaders (chap. 23), and eschatological teaching (chaps. 24–25). Scholars debate whether Matthew's famous Sermon on the Mount (chaps. 5–7) was a single sermon given by Jesus or is a representative collection of Jesus' teachings brought together by the author.

Structural Signals and Matthew's "Outline." In addition to fulfillment formulas and topical collections, various structural signals mark key transitions in Matthew's narrative. These provide clues to the overall structure of the Gospel. One such marker appears as a formula at the end of each of Jesus' five major discourses: *"And it came about when Jesus finished these words . . ."* (7:28; 11:1; 13:53; 19:1; 26:1). Matthew groups his narrative sections around these five discourses, providing a pattern of alternating narrative and discourse throughout the Gospel. Some have claimed that these five discourses were meant to parallel the five books of Moses (the Pentateuch) and so present the Gospel as a kind of "Christian Pentateuch," with Jesus as the new Moses.

A very different outline has been suggested by another structural signal, the phrase *"From that time Jesus began to . . ."* This formula appears twice, marking the beginning of Jesus' public ministry (4:17) and the beginning of his journey to Jerusalem to suffer and die (16:21). The resulting outline is similar to Mark's (see chapter 6), focusing on the identity (Matt. 1:1–4:16) and ministry (4:17–16:20) of the Messiah and then on his road to the cross (16:21–28:20).

So which represents Matthew's outline, the fivefold alternating discourses and narratives or the threefold progression of the narrative? There is probably not an either-or solution, since both features appear to be part of the author's plan. Ancient writers were probably not as concerned with a table of contents as writers are today, and Matthew may have used a variety of structural features simultaneously.

Matthew's Genealogy. Matthew begins his Gospel with a genealogy tracing the royal ancestry of Jesus (1:1–17). Modern readers often find genealogies strange, tedious, and even boring. The *Reader's Digest* condensation of the Bible eliminated most of them! But from Matthew's Jewish perspective, Jesus' genealogy is profoundly important, confirming his legitimacy as the promised savior and king who will bring Israel's history to its climax.

The author's love of organization is evident as he structures the genealogy into three sections of fourteen names: Abraham to David, David to the Babylonian exile, the Babylonian exile to the Messiah (1:17). The number fourteen may represent twice seven (the number of completion) or perhaps draws on the numerical value of the Hebrew name David. Since there are names known to be missing from Matthew's genealogy, it is clear that Matthew has intentionally abbreviated the list to fit this structure. This was a common practice in Jewish genealogies and was intended to develop a memorable structure or to emphasize certain individuals.

The structuring of the genealogy around Abraham, David, and the Babylonian exile is particularly significant. God had made a covenant with Abraham that all nations would be blessed through him (Gen. 12:2–3). He had made a covenant with David promising that one of David's descendants would reign forever on David's throne.

The Babylonian exile was viewed by Israel's prophets as punishment for the nation's sin and rebellion against God. Since the exile, no Davidic king had reigned in Israel, and many Jews of Jesus' day considered Israel still to be in exile, oppressed by the Gentiles and under God's judgment, awaiting the restoration of the Davidic dynasty by the Messiah. With his genealogy, Matthew announces that Jesus' birth marks the coming of the Messiah who will "save his people from their sins" (1:17, 21)—the very sins that caused the exile.

Matthew's genealogy is also unusual in its inclusion of five women—Tamar, Rahab, Ruth, the wife of Uriah (Bathsheba), and Mary the mother of Jesus—since women were not normally included in genealogies. Their significance is probably related to the fact that all were in some sense outsiders (sinners, outcasts, foreigners) whom God used to carry forward his saving purpose. They foreshadow the poor and lowly, the outcasts, and ultimately the Gentiles, who will respond to God's salvation.

The Sermon on the Mount. Matthew introduces Jesus' public ministry with the Sermon on the Mount (chaps. 5–7), a model of his preaching which sets the program for Jesus' kingdom proclamation. In the sermon, Jesus identifies himself as the true interpreter of the Old Testament law and the one who fulfills its purpose. As Moses went up to Mount Sinai to receive the first law, so Jesus goes up to a mountain to set forth its new formulation in the age of salvation. He has come not to abolish the law but to fulfill it, to bring it to its prophesied consummation (5:17). The old law written on stone is now superseded by the new law written on people's hearts (see Jer. 31:33). Jesus repeatedly clarifies the law of Moses, identifying its true intent and raising its standards to a higher plane. Whereas the Mosaic law forbade murder, Jesus now forbids even anger, which is murder committed in one's heart. Whereas the Mosaic law forbade adultery, the law of the kingdom forbids lust—adultery of the heart. These are new standards for the new age of salvation.

Questions for Review and Discussion

1. Who was Matthew, and what is the evidence that he wrote this Gospel?
2. To whom was Matthew's Gospel probably written and why?

3. What are some of the key literary and structural features of Matthew's Gospel?

Recommended Resources

Blomberg, Craig L. *Matthew*. New American Commentary. Nashville: Broadman, 1992.

Brown, Jeannine K. *Matthew*. Teach the Text Commentary Series. Grand Rapids: Baker, 2015.

France, R. T. *The Gospel of Matthew*. The New International Commentary on the New Testament. Grand Rapids: Eerdmans, 2007.

CHAPTER 5

THEMES AND THEOLOGY OF MATTHEW'S GOSPEL

MATTHEW'S PORTRAIT OF JESUS: THE GOSPEL OF THE MESSIAH

Jesus the Messiah. As noted in the previous chapter, Matthew begins with a genealogy identifying Jesus as "the Messiah the son of David, the son of Abraham" (1:1). Abraham and David are figures of great importance both in Israel's history and in Matthew's narrative purpose. Abraham was not only the father of the Jewish nation but also the recipient of the promise that all nations would be blessed through him (Gen. 12:2–3). The mission to the Gentiles in Matthew's day thus finds justification in the Abrahamic covenant (Matt. 8:11; 28:18–20). David was Israel's greatest king and the prototype of the coming Messiah. In the Davidic covenant, God promised that through David's "seed" (descendants) the messianic king would come (2 Sam. 7:12–16; Isa. 9:2–7; 11:1–16). As the Messiah (meaning "Anointed One"), Jesus is the promised king from David's line who will bring salvation to his people.

This royal messianic theme is also evident in Matthew's fondness for the title Son of David, which is applied to Jesus nine times in the Gospel (only three times each in Mark and Luke). In Judaism, this title often carried strong political connotations. Like the great warrior King David, the Son of David would lead God's people in victory over their enemies. Yet Matthew links the title especially to Jesus' humble presence (21:1–11) and compassionate healing ministry (9:27; 12:22–23; 15:22; 20:30–31; 21:14–15). Jesus' messiahship is revealed first not through conquest but through self-sacrificial love and service.

While the Davidic Messiah serves as Matthew's foundational category, it by no means exhausts his messianic portrait of Jesus. For Matthew, Jesus is also the Son of God, the Son of Man, the Suffering Servant, the new Moses, and the true Israel. What do all of these titles and typologies have in common? All are intimately connected to the Old Testament and to the theme of promise and fulfillment. For Matthew, Jesus fulfills it all: all of God's promises to and covenants with Abraham, Moses, and David. He is the climax of salvation history, the inaugurator of God's reign.

Immanuel: The Presence and Wisdom of God. While Matthew's portrait of Jesus may be called thoroughly messianic (relating to promise and fulfillment), there are also indications that Jesus' identity exceeds traditional messianic categories. In this regard, we may point to various "divine" or "transcendent" features of Matthew's Christology. From the start, the reader learns that Jesus is Immanuel— "God with us" (1:23). While this title could refer generally to Jesus as God's representative, there are indications that it carries a deeper significance, that Jesus is the very presence of God. In the Sermon on the Mount, Jesus quotes the Old Testament law, *"It has been said . . . ,"* then provides a clarification, *"but I tell you . . ."* The phrase echoes the authoritative Old Testament pronouncement "Thus says the LORD" and suggests that the words of Jesus are the words of God. Jesus also exercises functions and prerogatives traditionally associated with God. He forgives sins (9:2) and knows the thoughts of human beings (9:4; 12:25; 22:18). While affirming that people should worship God alone (4:10), he repeatedly accepts worship from others (2:11; 8:2; 9:18; 14:33; 15:25; 20:20; 28:9, 17).

Similarly, Jesus speaks and acts in ways that recall Old Testament language related to God. He sends prophets and wise men and teachers to Israel (Matt. 23:34). As God is a protective mother bird for his people (Ps. 17:8–9; 91:4; Isa. 31:5), so Jesus longs to gather Jerusalem to himself like a mother hen (Matt. 23:37). When the Son of Man comes to establish "his kingdom" (the kingdom of God), he will send "his angels" (God's angels) to gather the elect (Matt. 13:41; 24:31; cf. 15:31; 16:21, 28). At the final judgment, he will determine the eternal destiny of all human beings (25:31–46; 7:21–23). Perhaps most significant, in language reminiscent of the omnipresent Spirit of God in the Old Testament, Jesus promises his presence with his disciples whenever they gather in his name (18:20), even to the end of the age (28:20). While Matthew never explicitly identifies Jesus as God, the baptismal formula in 28:19 comes very close, placing him in relational equality with the Father and the Holy Spirit.

OTHER KEY THEMES

Promise Fulfillment and the Climax of Salvation History. All the major features of Matthew's Gospel—the genealogy, the fulfillment formulas, the titles of Jesus, the typologies—point to a common theme: *in Jesus, God has acted decisively to save his people.* The promises and covenants of the Old Testament are coming to fulfillment in him. The term *salvation history* is used to describe the narration or schematization of God's actions in human history to accomplish his salvation. Matthew's central theological theme is that *salvation history reaches its goal and purpose in Jesus the Messiah.* Matthew's presentation of salvation history is closely related to his perspective on the kingdom of God. In Jewish fashion, Matthew prefers the designation "kingdom of heaven" (thirty-two times) over "kingdom of God" (four times), with the circumlocution "heaven" replacing the divine name out of reverence. There seems to be no difference in meaning between the two expressions, and they often appear in identical contexts. God's kingdom in Matthew is both present and future. Inaugurated in the present, the kingdom will be consummated in the future when the Son of Man returns in glory to judge and reward.

Jesus and the Law. Jesus speaks more about the Old Testament law in Matthew than in the other Gospels. The issue of the nature of the law and its continuing validity was clearly an important one for Matthew and his community. One problem we encounter is that two seemingly contradictory perspectives appear side by side in Jesus' teaching. On the one hand, Jesus seems to teach the continuing authority of the law. Anyone who breaks the least of its commandments will be called least in the kingdom of heaven (5:18–19, 20, 48). On the other hand, Jesus makes statements that seem to abolish aspects of the law: "You have heard that it was said . . . But I tell you . . ." (Matt. 5:21–48). How can Jesus' teaching concerning the eternal validity of the law be reconciled with his statements that seem to overrule it?

Some scholars have suggested that Matthew is a moderate attempt to mediate between *antinomians*, those in the church who are rejecting the law altogether, and *legalists*, those who are preaching that Christians are still under the Mosaic law. While there may be some truth here, a better solution is to be found in Matthew's view of salvation history and the kingdom of God. Jesus announced that in his own words and deeds, the kingdom of God was breaking in on humanity. The age of promise was giving way to the age of fulfillment. With the new age comes a new covenant (Jer. 31:31; Matt. 26:28) and hence a new law. Citizens of the kingdom of heaven are no longer under the old covenant but under the new and greater covenant. As the inaugurator of the new covenant, Jesus claimed the prerogative to interpret, expand, and even overrule the law of Moses. Jesus has come not to abolish the law but to fulfill it (Matt. 5:17–18).

Under the new covenant, believers do not have a lower standard of righteousness but have a higher one, since the law is now written on their hearts rather than on tablets of stone (Jer. 31:33). This is why Jesus says that their righteousness must surpass that of the scribes and Pharisees (Matt. 5:20). This is also why Jesus defines the law as an attitude of the heart, not merely as the external command (5:22, 28). The whole law can be summed up in the commandments to love God and to love your neighbor (22:40), because the righteous actions which proceed from these two commands exceed the written standards of the Mosaic law.

The Jewish Leaders. While the disciples play a somewhat more positive role in Matthew than in Mark (see chapter 7), the religious leaders play a more negative one. While in Mark their primary character trait is that they *lack authority* and so are envious of Jesus' power and influence, in Matthew they are *evil* through and through (Matt. 9:4; 12:34, 39, 45; 16:4; 22:18). They are implacably opposed to Jesus and so are aligned with Satan, who himself is the "evil one" (5:37; 6:13; 13:19, 38). There is no hope for their redemption, since their hearts are thoroughly corrupt. This negative portrayal comes out in a variety of ways. Jesus and John the Baptist refer to them as a "brood of vipers" (3:7; 12:34; 23:33), and Jesus repeatedly calls them a "wicked and adulterous generation" (12:39; 16:4). The whole of chapter 23 concerns

Jesus' woes to, or denunciations against, the scribes and Pharisees for their hypocrisy, spiritual blindness, and evil deeds. Their characterization is epitomized in the parable of the wheat and the weeds, which appears only in Matthew (Matt. 13:24–30, 36–43). In that parable, the religious leaders are "people of the evil one," weeds sown by the devil among the good seed in the kingdom of God. Though they presently grow together with the good wheat, the righteous "people of the kingdom," in the end they will be weeded out and destroyed.

This negative portrayal of the religious leaders is likely a reflection of what is going on in Matthew's own church community, which is in intense and sometimes violent conflict with the larger Jewish community. Matthew's purpose is not only to demonstrate that Jesus is the Jewish Messiah but also to delegitimize his Jewish opponents. It is the church made up of Jews and Gentiles who are the true people of God in the present age.

The Great Commission. Matthew's Gospel ends with the Great Commission (28:18–20), which may be viewed as a thematic summary of the whole Gospel, bringing the plot to its resolution and carrying forward important themes. First, Jesus' *authority* to speak and act on God's behalf is now made universal and complete by virtue of his vindication in resurrection. Second, as in chapter 10, Jesus *delegates this authority to the disciples* to make disciples, baptize, and teach all he has commanded them. They are his representatives in the present age. Third, while the first mission of the disciples, in chapter 10, was only to Israel, now it is expanded to the whole world, *to make disciples of all nations.* Finally, the success of this worldwide mission is assured because *his absolute authority and abiding presence will sustain the disciples.* The Gospel which began with the announcement that Jesus is Immanuel, "God with us" (1:23), ends with the promise that he will be with his disciples till the end of the age (28:20).

READING MATTHEW TODAY

The modern reader often cringes when reading the strong language which Matthew uses against Jesus' Jewish opponents. The history of anti-Semitism, culminating with the Holocaust, makes these passages sound dangerously provocative. Indeed, through the centuries

Matthew's Gospel, like other New Testament passages, has been used to justify persecution of the Jews.

Yet to read these passages as anti-Semitic is to read them anachronistically ("out of their proper time"), and so to misread them. The Gospel is not an indictment of the Jews as a people. After all, Matthew and the majority of his church were Jewish! The Gospel is rather an internal debate within Judaism, between those who believe that Jesus is the promised Messiah and those who reject this claim. Matthew seeks to show that Jesus is the culmination of salvation history. God's purpose to bring salvation to lost humanity finds its culmination in him. The prophecies have been fulfilled! If Jesus is indeed the promised Messiah, then the church, which is made up of both Jews and Gentiles, is the authentic people of God. God's plan of salvation for the world is now going forward, not through the synagogue but through the new people of God made up of people from all nations. This is the critical point at issue for Matthew and his community.

Seen in this light, the questions Matthew answers are just as profound and important today. What is God's purpose and goal for this world? What characterizes the true followers of God? What must people do to find salvation? The first Gospel rejects any claims to truth that do not find their center in the kingdom of heaven inaugurated through the life, death, and resurrection of Jesus the Messiah. All other worldviews, religions, and philosophies fall short.

Questions for Review and Discussion

1. What two key themes characterize Matthew's portrait of Jesus?
2. To what central theme do all the major features of Matthew's Gospel point?
3. What is Matthew's perspective on the Jewish law?

Recommended Resources

France, R. T. *Matthew: Evangelist and Teacher.* Eugene, OR: Wipf and Stock, 2004.

Kingsbury, Jack Dean. *Matthew: Structure, Christology, Kingdom.* Minneapolis: Augsburg, 1991.

Luz, Ulrich. *The Theology of the Gospel of Matthew.* Cambridge: Cambridge Univ. Press, 1995.

CHAPTER 6

INTRODUCING MARK'S GOSPEL

I remember vividly January 17, 1991. It was the night the first Gulf War began with the launching of an allied air assault against Iraq. From their hotel in downtown Baghdad, CNN reporters Bernard Shaw and Peter Arnett gave a moment-by-moment report, describing the sounds of planes overhead and the sky lighting up with antiaircraft fire and bomb explosions. Those watching from around the world could not help but feel they were present in Baghdad, watching the war unfold before their eyes.

In many ways, Mark's Gospel has the same feel as an on-the-spot news report. The narrative is vivid, fast moving, and action packed. Jesus appears as the mighty Messiah and Son of God, moving through the Galilean countryside, exercising authority over friend and foe alike. He calls disciples, heals the sick, casts out demons, and teaches with great authority. There is a sense of awe and mystery about him, and amazement from those he encounters. Mark's lively story invites the reader to enter his narrative world and experience the coming of the Messiah, the arrival of God's promised salvation.

WHO WROTE MARK'S GOSPEL?

Like the other three Gospels, Mark's Gospel does not name its author. The title "According to Mark" *(kata Markon)* was probably added when the Gospels were brought together into a collection. Despite this anonymity, there is good reason to believe that the author was John Mark.

The early church historian Eusebius, writing in the fourth century AD, quotes the church leader Papias, who affirmed that "Mark became the interpreter of Peter" and wrote his version of the gospel. Papias, who was the bishop of Hierapolis in Asia Minor till about AD 130, claims that he received this information from the elder John, probably a reference to the apostle John. This would take the tradition back to the first generation of believers. Other early church writers affirm that Mark was the author of this Gospel and that he was dependent on the eyewitness accounts of Peter.

Who was this Mark? While Mark was a common name in the first century, only one figure in the New Testament appears as a likely candidate. John Mark was the son of a woman named Mary, in whose house the Jerusalem church met (Acts 12:12). As a young man, Mark accompanied his cousin Barnabas and the apostle Paul on their first missionary journey (Acts 13:5). For unknown reasons, he left the missionary group at Perga in Pamphylia and returned to Jerusalem (Acts 13:13). Because of this desertion, Paul refused to take Mark on his second journey. A rift developed between Paul and Barnabas, and the two separated, with Barnabas taking Mark and sailing to Cyprus, while Paul chose Silas and returned to Galatia (Acts 15:36–41). Despite this division, we know Mark and Paul were eventually reconciled, since Paul refers to him as his "coworker," or "fellow worker," in letters written ten years later (Col. 4:10–11; Philem. 24). Mark's value to Paul is also evident in 2 Timothy 4:11, where Paul tells Timothy to bring Mark with him to Rome because he is "helpful to me in my ministry."

While Mark is most closely associated with Paul in the New Testament, the early church tradition that he also worked closely with Peter finds support in 1 Peter 5:13, where Peter sends greetings from "my son Mark." Peter is probably referring to Mark as his disciple, or spiritual son. What Papias means when he says that Mark became Peter's "interpreter" is debated. Some believe that Peter normally preached in Aramaic and Mark served as his Greek interpreter. Others think that the term refers to the task of putting Peter's oral preaching into written form.

WHERE WAS MARK'S GOSPEL WRITTEN?

Early church tradition claims that Mark wrote from Rome to a Roman Christian audience. This agrees with New Testament references that place Mark in Rome with both Paul (Col. 4:10; Philem. 24; cf. 2 Tim. 4:11) and Peter (1 Peter 5:13, where "Babylon" is probably a cryptic reference to Rome).

A Roman location also fits well with material found in the Gospel. Mark translates Aramaic expressions for a Greek-speaking audience (3:17; 5:41; 7:34; 14:36; 15:34) and explains Jewish customs for Gentile readers (7:2–4; 15:42). Mark also explains Greek expressions by their Latin equivalents (see 12:42, where Jewish currency ["two *lepta*"] is explained by its Roman equivalence ["a *quadrans*"]). Although Greek was spoken throughout the empire, Latin was primarily used in Rome and Italy. Another bit of incidental evidence for Rome comes from 15:21, where Rufus and Alexander are named as the sons of Simon of Cyrene, presumably because they were known by Mark's church. This could be the same Rufus identified by Paul as a member of the Roman church (Rom. 16:13). Finally, the Gospel's special interest in persecution and martyrdom would fit well with a Roman audience, since the Roman church was a persecuted group of believers.

WHEN WAS MARK'S GOSPEL WRITTEN?

The date of Mark is uncertain. Some evidence points to an early date in the AD 50s or 60s. Clement of Alexandria claimed Mark wrote his Gospel while Peter was ministering in Rome. Since Peter is in Jerusalem in Acts 15, around AD 49, he probably came to Rome after this date, perhaps in the early 50s. If Peter was martyred during the persecutions of the emperor Nero around AD 64–67, this would allow for a date anytime from the mid-50s to the early 60s.

Other scholars prefer a date in the late 60s. The church father Irenaeus differs from Clement by claiming that Mark wrote his Gospel after the departure of Peter and Paul. If "departure" means death, which seems likely, Mark's Gospel would have been written in the late 60s or in the 70s. A date in the late 60s may also be suggested by Mark 13:14, where in the middle of Jesus' discourse on the Mount of Olives, the author adds a cryptic comment: "let the reader understand." Since the discourse refers to the destruction of Jerusalem (13:2), the comment may indicate that at the time of writing, the Jewish War of AD 66–73 had already begun.

WHY WAS MARK'S GOSPEL WRITTEN?

What prompted Mark to write this powerful and fast-paced Gospel? We can suggest at least three purposes. The first is *historical*. As the original apostles began to pass from the scene, Mark sought to record for generations to come their testimony about Jesus. Mark realized that what had been primarily an oral proclamation needed to be written down.

A second purpose is *christological* and *apologetic*. Mark writes to defend who Jesus is and what he came to accomplish. From a human perspective, Jesus was a complete failure. He was rejected by his own people. He suffered crucifixion, the most shameful and humiliating death imaginable, at the hands of the Roman authorities. The kingdom he announced apparently did not arrive. Mark writes to show that Jesus was who he claimed to be—the Messiah—and that through his life, death, and resurrection he has accomplished our salvation.

Mark's overall structure emphasizes this apologetic purpose. The first half of the Gospel (1:1–8:29) demonstrates that Jesus is the mighty Messiah and Son of God (1:1). Jesus acts with extraordinary authority, healing the sick, casting out demons, raising the dead, exercising authority over the forces of nature. All these acts confirm that he is indeed God's Messiah and agent of salvation. Yet when Peter, the key representative of the disciples, confesses that Jesus is the Messiah, Jesus radically redefines the role of the Messiah as suffering and dying as a sacrifice for sins (8:27–33; 9:31; 10:33–34, 45). For the rest of the Gospel (8:30–16:8), Jesus prepares his disciples for his suffering role and heads to Jerusalem to suffer and die. Mark's crucial point is that Jesus is not here to destroy the Roman legions; he is here to defeat much greater and more powerful foes: Satan, sin, and death. Jesus has come to reverse the results of the fall.

A third purpose relates to this second, in that the Gospel is a *practical call to follow Jesus in cross-bearing discipleship*. Mark wrote to challenge his readers that true discipleship means following the path of Jesus through suffering to glory.

As noted previously, this challenge may be related to the persecution of the church in Rome instigated by the emperor Nero. This began in AD 64 after a terrible fire destroyed more than half the city of Rome. When rumors began circulating that the emperor had ordered the fire as a means of "urban renewal," Nero shifted the blame to the Christians. Already viewed with suspicion, Christians were persecuted with terrible cruelty. The Roman historian Tacitus describes their horrible suffering: some were crucified; others were sewn into animal skins and hunted by dogs; still others were covered with pitch and burned at night as torches. Mark's emphasis on the need to suffer for Christ would fit this period of intense persecution. Another possibility is that the allusions to persecution reflect an earlier period and are linked to riots between Jews and Jewish Christians in AD 49–50. These disputes prompted the emperor Claudius to expel the Jewish population from Rome (Acts 18:2). The theme of suffering and persecution could then fit either the earlier or later dates suggested for the Gospel.

LITERARY FEATURES OF MARK'S GOSPEL

Fast-Paced Style. Mark's Gospel has a fast-moving narrative style. The narrator is fond of the Greek word *euthys*, an adverb often translated "immediately." It appears forty-two times, whereas Matthew uses it only five times and Luke only once. While the word does not always mean "just then," its effect is to propel the narrative forward.

The narrator also uses present-tense verbs to describe past actions, a Greek idiom known as the *historical present* (151 times; Matthew 93 times; Luke 11 times). The historical present also gives the narrative a vivid and realistic feel, like a newscaster giving an on-the-spot report. Retaining the present tense of these verbs, the account of Jesus' calming of the sea would read, "Leaving the crowd, they are taking him along with them in the boat. . . . There is arising a fierce gale of wind . . . and they are waking him and saying to him . . ." (Mark 4:36–38, my trans.).

Intercalation, or "Sandwiching." One of the most distinctive features of Mark's rhetoric is the literary device known as intercalation, the sandwiching of one event between the beginning and end of another. The two events are related to the same theme and serve to interpret one another. For example, Mark sandwiches Jesus' cleansing of the temple between his cursing of a fig tree and the disciples' later discovery of the withered tree (11:12–25). The intercalation suggests that the withering, like the temple clearing, represents God's judgment against Israel for its unbelief.

Triads, or Sets of Three. Mark is fond of patterns of three, or triads. Three boat scenes illustrate the disciples' lack of faith and comprehension (4:35–41; 6:45–52; 8:14–21). In three cycles of events, Jesus predicts his death and then teaches his disciples about servant leadership (8:31–38; 9:31–37; 10:32–45). In his eschatological sermon on the Mount of Olives, Jesus three times calls his disciples to alertness (13:33, 35, 37); in Gethsemane, he three times finds them sleeping (14:37, 40, 41). Peter denies Jesus three times (14:68, 70, 71), and three time references are mentioned during the crucifixion (15:25, 33, 34). Like a good preacher, the narrator uses repetition to drive his point home.

Irony. Because Mark's central theological theme—the Messiah who suffers—is itself paradoxical, irony plays a major role in the narrative. Much of this is situational irony. Jesus' opponents inadvertently speak ironically. They accuse Jesus of being in league with Satan (3:22), when in fact *they* are opposing God's kingdom. Seeking to trap Jesus through flattery, they call him a man of integrity who teaches the true way of God (12:13–14). While they do not believe this, ironically the reader knows that it is true. These same leaders mock Jesus on the cross, saying, "He saved others . . . but he can't save himself . . . this Messiah, this king of Israel" (15:31–32). Their sarcastic comments are in fact true. Jesus is both savior and king. Though the religious elite of Israel reject Jesus as the Son of God, a Gentile centurion recognizes it (15:39). Throughout the Gospel, the spiritual insiders of Israel—the religious leaders—become the outsiders in the kingdom of God, and the spiritual outsiders—sinners, tax collectors, Gentiles—become the insiders. It is ironic that blind Bartimaeus sees that Jesus is the Son of David (10:46–52), but his religious opponents are spiritually blind.

There is also much verbal irony in the Gospel. Jesus quotes an ironic proverb: "A prophet is not without honor except in his own town" (6:4). Ironic sarcasm is evident as he congratulates the religious leaders for setting aside the commandments of God in favor of their own traditions (7:9).

Questions for Review and Discussion

1. What do we know about John Mark from the New Testament?
2. Where was Mark's Gospel likely written, and how does this relate to its main themes?
3. What were Mark's primary purposes in writing?
4. Describe Mark's literary style. What is intercalation? What are triads?

Recommended Resources

France, R. T. *The Gospel of Mark*. The New International Greek Testament Commentary. Grand Rapids: Eerdmans, 2002.

Stein, Robert. *Mark*. Baker Exegetical Commentary on the New Testament. Grand Rapids: Baker, 2008.

Strauss, Mark L. *Mark*. Exegetical Commentary on the New Testament. Grand Rapids: Zondervan, 2014.

CHAPTER 7

THEMES AND THEOLOGY OF MARK'S GOSPEL

MARK'S PORTRAIT OF JESUS: MIGHTY MESSIAH AND SUFFERING SERVANT

The primary purpose of Mark's high-speed narrative is to portray Jesus as the mighty Messiah and Son of God, a theme that dominates the first half of the Gospel (chaps. 1–8). Jesus' central message—"The kingdom of God has come near" (1:14–15)—is itself a demonstration of authority. Through his words and deeds, the longed-for reign of God is breaking into human history. Everything Jesus does, he does with authority. When he calls four fishermen to follow him—men immersed in lives, families, and livelihoods—they leave everything to follow him (1:16–20). Jesus also teaches with great authority (1:22, 27) and exercises authority over natural and supernatural enemies alike. He heals the sick, casts out demons, and raises the dead. He controls the forces of nature, calming the storm and feeding thousands with a few loaves and fishes. The purpose of these miracles is *not* to gain popularity but to demonstrate that he is acting and speaking with the authority of God. Most profound, Jesus claims prerogatives of God alone. He forgives sins (2:5), discerns the thoughts of his opponents (2:8), claims lordship over the Sabbath (2:28), and apparently overrules Old Testament dietary laws (7:18–19).

The narrator emphasizes this sense of authority by noting the awed reactions of those who encounter Jesus. The people are amazed at his teaching (1:22, 27; 11:18) and astonished at his exorcisms and healing power (1:27; 2:12; 5:20; 6:2; 7:37). The disciples express awe when he raises the dead and calms the sea (5:42; 6:51). His popularity grows and grows (1:33, 37, 45; 2:2; 3:7–10; 5:24).

The question of Jesus' identity is raised implicitly throughout the first half of Mark's Gospel. It comes to center stage in the account of the calming of the storm, when the astonished disciples ask, "Who is this? Even the wind and the waves obey him!" (4:41). The answer, of course, has already been given: Jesus is the Messiah and the Son of God. The reader already knows this (1:1); the Father has announced it to the Son (1:11); Satan and his demonic forces know it (1:24, 34). Yet the narrative reaches its midpoint and initial climax when the first human character proclaims it. The confession of Peter at Caesarea Philippi marks a key turning point as the chief representative of the disciples recognizes Jesus to be the Messiah, God's agent of salvation (8:27–29). Jesus' authoritative words and deeds have confirmed that he is indeed the one to accomplish Israel's salvation.

The reader is shocked, however, when Jesus commands the disciples to silence and then teaches them that his role as Messiah is to suffer and die (8:30–31). While Jesus' rejection and death have been hinted at earlier in the narrative (2:20; 3:6; 6:4), from this point on, his suffering mission becomes the primary focus (chaps. 8–15). Three times Jesus predicts his death (8:31; 9:31; 10:33–34). Each time the disciples fail to get it, responding with pride and incomprehension (8:32; 9:33–34; 10:35–41). Three times Jesus must teach that the true path of discipleship is one of suffering and sacrifice (8:33–38; 9:35–37; 10:42–45).

The third of these triads comes in chapter 10. Jesus begins his journey to Jerusalem and announces for a third time that he is going there to suffer and die. James and John demonstrate pride by asking for the best seats in the kingdom; the other disciples respond with indignation (10:35–41). For a third time, Jesus must teach a lesson in humble servanthood: those who wish to be great must become the servants and slaves of all (10:42–45). Mark 10:45 has rightly been called the theme verse for the Gospel: "Even the Son of Man did not come to be served, but to serve, and to give his life as a ransom for many." The verse echoes the role of the Servant of the LORD— described by Isaiah—who suffers an atoning death for the sins of the nation (Isa. 52:13–53:12). As the narrative turns toward its climax, the reader is reminded that the Messiah must first pass through suffering and sacrifice on his way to glory.

OTHER KEY THEMES

The Kingdom of God. Jesus' central message in Mark concerns the coming of the kingdom of God. When Jesus' ministry begins, he announces, "The kingdom of God has come near" (1:15). But what is the nature of this kingdom, and in what sense is it arriving? On the one hand, God's kingdom could refer to God's sovereign authority over creation. God always has been and always will be King of the universe. Yet on the other hand, God's authority has been compromised because of human sin and rebellion. The apocalyptic Judaism of Jesus' day acknowledged the present reality of God's sovereign authority but placed greatest emphasis on the future coming of the kingdom. The persecuted people of God longed for the day when God would intervene in human history to judge the wicked and reign as sovereign over all the earth.

Jesus' proclamation of the kingdom meant that this intervention—the restoration of God's reign and the renewal of fallen creation—was arriving through his own words and actions. Yet God's reign would be accomplished not through the physical conquest of Israel's enemies but through Jesus' death and resurrection, when he would break the power of Satan, sin, and death. Jesus' miracles—healings, exorcisms, and nature miracles—were symbols or previews of this restoration of creation.

Though inaugurated through Jesus' life, death, and resurrection, the kingdom will be consummated—brought to complete fulfillment—when the Son of Man returns in power and glory. Jesus' kingdom teaching in Mark contains both present and future elements. Jesus speaks of those who in the future will see the kingdom of God come with power (9:1) and refers to a future time when he will drink wine again in the kingdom of God (14:25). Joseph of Arimathea is longing for the kingdom of God (15:43), and at the triumphal entry, the people express their hope in "the coming kingdom of our father David" (11:10). Jesus speaks of the time when the Son of Man will come "with great power and glory" to "gather his elect" (13:26–32; cf. 8:38; 13:33–34; 14:62).

At the same time, there are present dimensions to the kingdom. The parable of the growing seed describes the kingdom as the slow growth from seed to plant until the day of harvest (4:26–29). Similarly, the parable of the mustard seed represents the kingdom as a tiny seed that grows into a great tree (4:30–32). In both parables, the kingdom is something that begins with Jesus' ministry and is consummated at his return.

Discipleship: Following the Servant's Suffering Path. Another major theme of Mark's Gospel is authentic discipleship. True followers of Jesus must be willing to take up their cross and follow him, even to suffering and death (8:34). If Jesus is the main protagonist and the religious leaders are antagonists, the disciples play a more ambiguous role in Mark's narrative. On the one hand, these men hold a privileged position in Jesus' ministry. Jesus personally seeks them out and calls them to be his disciples. From among his many followers, he appoints twelve to be his special "apostles" (3:13–19; 6:30). The number twelve is surely significant, identifying these as leaders among the restored remnant of the twelve tribes of Israel. Having chosen them as his representatives, Jesus places great trust in them and sends them out with extraordinary authority to proclaim his message of the kingdom and to cast out demons (6:7–13, 30).

On the other hand, despite this special status and responsibility, in Mark's Gospel the Twelve are examples of failure more often than of success. Of the four Gospels, Mark's portrait of the disciples is the most negative. They repeatedly fail to understand Jesus' teaching (4:13; 7:18) and to recognize his authoritative power (6:37, 52; 8:4). They cannot comprehend the true nature of his messiahship (8:32; 9:32). They act with pride and from self-interest (9:38; 10:13, 37, 41). Jesus repeatedly rebukes them for their failure to understand his teaching and for their lack of faith (4:13, 40; 7:18; 9:19).

Critical to the disciples' failure is their unwillingness to recognize the suffering role of the Messiah. As noted previously, the narrator drives this home with three cycles of failures, in which Jesus predicts his death, the disciples respond with pride and incomprehension, and Jesus teaches on servant leadership (8:31–38; 9:31–37; 10:32–45).

Unlike the other Gospels, Mark does not describe the recovery of the disciples. When Jesus is arrested, they flee in terror. Judas betrays Jesus. Peter denies him three times. No one comes to his defense. No account is given of the disciples' restoration after the resurrection. The narrator's purpose seems to be to set the example of Jesus in contrast to that of the disciples. While he remains faithful, they are faithless. While he perseveres, they collapse and run. In this sense, Mark's disciples function almost as anti-disciples, revealing to the reader how followers of Jesus should not behave. Jesus himself becomes the model of true discipleship, doing the Father's will even through suffering and death.

A Puzzling Ending. Mark's resurrection account is one of the most puzzling parts of his Gospel. The problem is that the earliest and most reliable manuscripts do not contain verses 9–20, ending instead with verse 8. This seems like an odd way to end the Gospel. The women visit the tomb, where a young man dressed in white reports that Jesus has risen from the dead. He tells them to report this to the disciples, who should go to Galilee, where they will see Jesus. The final verse says that the women fled trembling and bewildered and said nothing to anyone. The reader is left wondering what this means. Did the women ever recover from their fear and tell the disciples? Did the disciples go to Galilee and see Jesus? Why are no resurrection appearances reported?

If verses 9–20 are not part of the original Gospel, as most scholars agree, there are two possibilities. Some scholars believe that the original ending was somehow lost in the transmission process. If this is the case, the last section may have looked something like Matthew 28:16–20, which includes Jesus' appearance to the disciples in Galilee. Other scholars, however, believe that the abrupt ending of the Gospel was no accident but that the author intended to end the story this way. According to this view, the sense of mystery and awe that runs through the entire Gospel also characterizes the resurrection account. The women are left not with resurrection appearances but with the empty tomb and the announcement of the risen Lord. Like the characters in the narrative, the reader must decide how to respond to this proclamation—with faith or with fear.

This is not to say that the author did not know about the resurrection appearances. He surely knew that Jesus' disciples saw him alive, recovered from their failure, and became the foundation of the apostolic church (see 13:9–11; 14:28; 16:7). The angel's command to go to Galilee would be inexplicable unless the disciples later saw Jesus there. But these historical events have no part in the narrative. The narrator rather leaves readers with the proclamation of the resurrection and an implicit call to faith and decision. Will they, like Jesus, face suffering and trials with faithfulness, or will they flee and deny him, like the disciples? The resolution (or perhaps irresolution) of the plot calls the reader to decision.

READING MARK TODAY

One day some time ago, I was flipping through a Christian magazine, reading articles on the kinds of things American Christians tend to fight over: the nature of church governance, issues of church and state, theological debates about eschatology and spiritual gifts. I casually turned a page, and there before me was a gruesome picture of two bodies, bloody and badly mutilated. In the context of my "light" reading, it startled me. I read the caption describing Christian martyrs in Indonesia. The picture showed their enemies beating their lifeless bodies. Later that day, an email crossed my desk. It told of an Australian missionary and his two young sons who were burned alive in their car in India by an angry mob. These were sobering moments. As I sat in my comfortable office, in the safety of my middle-class community, in a nation of peace and prosperity, these images brought home the sobering reality that many Christians around the world are suffering and dying for their faith.

Mark's Gospel reminds us that the goal of the Christian life is not to find security or self-fulfillment. Following Jesus is responding to a radical call to commitment, taking up our crosses and following him. The gospel holds no promise for those who are seeking power and wealth and fame and prestige. To be first, Jesus says, you must be last. To be a leader, you must become a slave. To live, you must die.

The gospel begins with the startling announcement that the reign of God, his sovereign authority, has arrived through the powerful words and deeds of Jesus the Messiah. The glories of God's kingdom are available to all who will receive it. Yet startlingly, the king does not conquer but rather dies. His followers are scattered and bewildered. Even the announcement of the resurrection brings puzzlement and fear. This is "good news"?

Comprehending Mark's Gospel requires a paradigm shift for the modern reader. It requires us to see beyond the present world, where tyrants still rule and oppressors still oppress. The good news of salvation is that Jesus' death, though seemingly a defeat, was a spiritual victory of cosmic proportions. Satan and sin and death are now defeated. The age to come has broken into human history and is now available to those who receive it.

Paradoxically, receiving the kingdom means dying to self and living for God. It means giving up efforts to earn God's favor and receiving his free gift of grace. In our age, in which human accomplishment and personal fulfillment are considered the highest of life's goals, Mark's Gospel calls us to radical faith and self-denial. Relationships are now defined not through the bonds of family or culture or ethnicity but rather through spiritual identity: our brothers and sisters are those who do the will of God (Mark 3:35). As the people of God living simultaneously in the present evil age and the age to come, believers are called to alertness and anticipation for the return of the Son of Man and to willing submission to follow his path of suffering.

Questions for Review and Discussion

1. How is Jesus presented in the two halves of Mark's Gospel? What is the key turning point?
2. What are Mark's main theological themes?
3. What role do the disciples play, and how does this relate to Mark's theme of discipleship?

Recommended Resources

Best, Ernest. *Following Jesus: Discipleship in the Gospel of Mark.* JSNT Supplement 4. Sheffield: JSOT Press, 1988.

Garland, David. *A Theology of Mark's Gospel: Good News about Jesus the Messiah, the Son of God.* Grand Rapids: Zondervan, 2015.

Harrington, Daniel. *What Are They Saying about Mark?* Mahwah, NJ: Paulist, 2005.

CHAPTER 8

INTRODUCING LUKE'S GOSPEL

In 1871, French archeologist Charles Clermont-Ganneau discovered a plaque which once stood at the entrance to the Jerusalem temple. The plaque, written in Greek, reads, "No outsider shall enter the protective enclosure around the sanctuary. And whoever is caught will only have himself to blame for the ensuing death." The inscription well illustrates the exclusive nature of Judaism in the first century, when Gentiles were forbidden from entering the temple of God upon pain of death. Luke's Gospel and its companion volume, Acts, boldly announce that this time of exclusion is past. The fulfillment of God's promises through Jesus' life, death, resurrection, and ascension means that all people everywhere—whether Jew or Gentile, slave or free, male or female—now have access to God's salvation. By fulfilling the promises made to Israel, Jesus the Messiah has become the Savior for all people.

LUKE-ACTS, A TWO-VOLUME WORK

Luke is unique among the Gospels in that it has a sequel—the book of Acts—which narrates the events of the early church following Jesus' death and resurrection. There is near universal agreement that Luke and Acts were written by the same author, since they share a common style, theology, and addressee (Theophilus). Furthermore, it is widely acknowledged today that not only do they have the same author, but they are a literary unity—a single two-volume work. At the beginning of Acts (1:1–2), the author refers back to the Gospel: "In my former book, Theophilus, I wrote about all that Jesus began to do and to teach until the day he was taken up to heaven." If the

Gospel is what Jesus *began to do and to teach*, then Acts is what he *continues to do* through the establishment and spread of his church in the power of the Holy Spirit, whom he has poured out. The hyphenated expression "Luke-Acts" is used to describe this two-volume work.

WHO WROTE LUKE'S GOSPEL?

Early church tradition unanimously ascribes these two works to Luke, a physician and part-time companion of the apostle Paul. This external evidence can be supplemented with internal evidence. Several times in Acts, the author uses the first-person plural "we," indicating that he traveled with Paul during his second and third missionary journeys and eventually went with him to Rome (16:10–17; 20:5–21; 21:1–18; 27:1–28:16). From the letters of Paul, we know that Luke was a companion of Paul and was with him in Rome (Col. 4:7–17; Philem. 23–24; cf. 2 Tim. 4:10–11).

The author claims not to have been an eyewitness of what he wrote in the Gospel but rather to have thoroughly investigated the events before composing his work (Luke 1:1–4). Tradition tells us that Luke was a converted Gentile. This agrees with Colossians 4:11–14, where Paul distinguishes Luke from his Jewish companions. This would help to explain the author's keen interest in the Gentile reception of the gospel. Luke's exceptional knowledge of Judaism and the Old Testament suggests that before following Christ, he may have been a "God-fearer," a Gentile worshiper of the God of Israel.

Luke's Gospel is the longest book in the New Testament. Together with Acts, it comprises the largest amount of material by a New Testament author (even more than Paul's!). Luke also begins earlier (with the announcement of John's birth) and ends later (with Jesus' ascension) than the other Synoptics.

WHEN WAS LUKE'S GOSPEL WRITTEN?

The date of the Gospel is closely tied to its companion volume Acts. Since Paul is in prison in Rome at the end of Acts (about AD 62), Luke may have finished Acts before Paul's release and later martyrdom. This would place Acts around AD 62, and the Gospel even earlier.

On the other hand, if Mark was the first Gospel written and was composed shortly before the destruction of Jerusalem (mid- to late 60s; see Mark 13:14), Luke and Acts would have come later, from the late 60s onward. In this case, Luke could have a different reason for ending Luke-Acts with Paul in Rome, perhaps to show that the Gospel had reached "the ends of the earth" (Acts 1:8).

Some have said the book must be dated after AD 70, since Luke's description of the siege and destruction of Jerusalem is more detailed than Mark's and must have been written after the fact (Luke 21:20–24). This conclusion begins with the invalid assumption that Jesus could not have predicted the future. Even for those seeking a natural explanation it is unsatisfactory, since Luke's description of the destruction is quite general and could apply to almost any Roman siege. Without more evidence, the date of Luke-Acts remains an open question.

TO WHOM WAS LUKE'S GOSPEL WRITTEN?

Who was this Theophilus to whom Luke and Acts are addressed? The name means "one who loves God," and some claim Luke is writing generally to believers. More likely, Theophilus is an individual, probably the patron who sponsored Luke's writing. The composition of a book of this length was an expensive endeavor in the ancient world, and it was common to dedicate such a work to an influential patron. The address "most excellent" indicates Theophilus's high social or political status. Luke's claim to be providing "certainty" concerning "the things you have been taught" may suggest that Theophilus is a new Christian needing instruction, or an interested unbeliever. Apart from these observations, his identity remains a mystery.

Though dedicated to Theophilus, the Gospel and Acts are almost certainly intended for a wider audience, perhaps the church or churches with which Luke and Theophilus are associated. Yet the specific provenance (place of origin) and destination remain a mystery. Many suggestions have been made (Rome, Philippi, Achaia, Antioch), but little evidence can be marshaled for any of them.

WHY WAS LUKE'S GOSPEL WRITTEN?

We are on firmer ground concerning the purpose for which Luke wrote. He states that, having investigated everything carefully, he is confirming for Theophilus "the certainty of the things you have been taught" (Luke 1:1–4). Luke writes to confirm the gospel—to demonstrate the authenticity of the claims of Christianity. This confirmation certainly relates to accusations made by the church's Jewish opponents. The author takes pains to show that Jesus is the Jewish Messiah, that it was God's purpose for him to suffer, die, and rise again, that the mission to the Gentiles was ordained and instigated by God, and that Paul is not a renegade Jew but a faithful servant of the Lord. There are also indications that Luke seeks to deflect Roman criticism. Both Jesus (in the Gospel) and Paul (in Acts) are repeatedly confirmed as innocent of Roman charges. Christianity is not a dangerous new religion but the fulfillment of Judaism, the consummation of God's plan of salvation.

The diversity of Luke's work suggests that he is writing for a variety of reasons: to teach believers about the origin of their faith, to defend Christianity against its opponents, and to establish a firm historical foundation for the gospel now advancing around the world.

LITERARY FEATURES OF LUKE'S GOSPEL

Historiography. Luke shows a strong interest in history writing, claiming to be drawing from eyewitness accounts and to have carefully investigated these events (1:1–4). He dates the Gospel with reference to Roman history, identifying key rulers and religious leaders (cf. 1:5; 2:1–3; 3:1–2). Luke is clearly interested in showing the historical veracity and worldwide significance of these events.

Fine Literary Style. Luke's two books represent some of the best Greek in the New Testament. The author is clearly a skilled literary artist, able to adapt his style to fit the occasion. Luke's Gospel begins with a formal prologue similar in style to that of Hellenistic writers of the first century. These verses contain some of the finest literary Greek in the Bible. Yet as the reader moves from Luke's formal introduction to the birth narrative, the writing style changes dramatically.

The language suddenly takes on an archaic sound reminiscent of the Septuagint, the Greek Old Testament. For the modern reader, it would be something like beginning a story with "Once upon a time . . ." or dropping into a King James style of English. Judging from the author's literary skills, this stylistic change would seem to be intentional and serves to transport the reader into the world of the Old Testament.

Luke's Birth Narrative. Only Matthew and Luke include accounts of Jesus' birth (Matthew 1–2; Luke 1–2). These birth stories are not intended merely to provide the curious reader with details about Jesus' birth. They serve rather as overtures for the symphony that follows, setting the tone for the rest of each Gospel. Both birth narratives focus on the themes of promise and fulfillment and the arrival of messianic salvation. Jesus is the promised Messiah, the descendant of David born to be king. His coming is the fulfillment of Jewish hopes. In Luke, parallels and motifs from the Old Testament abound. The characters we encounter—Zechariah, Elizabeth, Mary, Joseph, Simeon, Anna— are models of Jewish piety. The narrator's purpose is to introduce the reader to the faithful remnant of the people of God, waiting expectantly for the fulfillment of the promises God has made to them.

The central theme of Luke's birth narrative is *the arrival of God's salvation and the fulfillment of his promises to Israel*. Two structural features help to carry this theme forward. The first is the parallel accounts of the births of Jesus and John. The two stories are intertwined, with similar announcements by the angel Gabriel and parallel accounts of Jesus' and John's birth, circumcision, and naming. The narrator's purpose is twofold, both to *link* Jesus and John as coagents of God's salvation and to *distinguish* their status and roles. While John will be "a prophet of the Most High" (1:76), Jesus is "the Son of the Most High" (1:32). John's birth to a barren woman is miraculous, but Jesus' birth to a virgin is unique and unprecedented. John's role is to prepare the way for the Lord (1:17), but Jesus *is* that Lord—the Savior, who is Christ the Lord (2:11). Like others in the narrative, John prepares the way for Jesus and bears testimony that he is the Messiah and Savior of the world.

A second structural feature of the birth narrative is the series of birth narrative "hymns," or songs of praise, offered up by Spirit-filled characters in the drama. These hymns, which resemble Old Testament psalms, function much like the songs in a modern musical play. Just as the characters in *Oklahoma!* or *My Fair Lady* suddenly break into song, explaining or elaborating on the story, so Mary (1:46–55), Zechariah (1:67–79), and Simeon (2:29–32) break into Spirit-inspired celebration of God's salvation.

The Nazareth Sermon. One of the most theologically important passages in Luke's Gospel is the Nazareth sermon (4:14–30), Jesus' inaugural sermon in his hometown in Galilee. Luke moves this important episode forward from its later position in Mark (6:1–6) to serve as a summarizing introduction for Jesus' ministry. Jesus participates in the synagogue service, reading Isaiah 61 and applying it to himself, essentially declaring himself to be God's Messiah: "The Spirit of the Lord is on me, because he has anointed me to proclaim good news to the poor. He has sent me to proclaim freedom for the prisoners and recovery of sight for the blind, to set the oppressed free, to proclaim the year of the Lord's favor" (4:18–19, citing Isaiah 61:1–2; 58:6).

This message of freedom and hope would have struck a chord with the people of Nazareth, who saw themselves as the poor and oppressed whose deliverance Jesus announced. Yet Jesus shocks his audience by pointing out that in the past, God favored Gentiles like the widow of Zarephath and Naaman the Syrian over the people of Israel. Enraged, the townspeople drive Jesus out of town and attempt to throw him off a cliff. Jesus walks through the crowd and escapes.

The sermon is significant because it plays out in miniature the story that will unfold in the Gospel. Jesus' rejection in Nazareth foreshadows his coming rejection by his own people Israel. His announcement that "no prophet is accepted in his hometown" (v. 24) becomes a prediction of his death in Jerusalem. Yet through his resurrection, he will provide spiritual deliverance for Jew and Gentile alike.

The Travel Narrative. Perhaps the most unique structural feature of Luke's Gospel is the extended journey to Jerusalem, or "travel narrative," from 9:51 to 19:27. At Luke 9:51, following Peter's confession and the transfiguration, Luke says that Jesus "resolutely set out for Jerusalem." The author then takes ten chapters to treat a period which in Mark's Gospel occupies a single chapter. What is unusual about this "journey" is that Jesus does not head straight for

Jerusalem but wanders from place to place. Though notices in the text occasionally remind the reader that Jesus is traveling or that he is heading for Jerusalem, the bulk of the material is not a travel itinerary at all but teachings of Jesus together with a few miracle stories. In short, the journey is not a straight-line trip to Jerusalem but *a period of Jesus' heightened resolve* to reach his Jerusalem goal. Here we see the key symbolic and theological role of Jerusalem in Luke's work. It is in Jerusalem where the prophets were killed, and there God will accomplish his salvation (13:32–35).

Many of the stories and parables in this section concern God's special care for the poor and outcast. For this reason, this section has sometimes been called the *Gospel for the Outcast* (9:51–19:27). Well-known parables include the good Samaritan (10:25–37), the rich fool (12:13–21), the great banquet (14:15–24), things lost (sheep, coin, and son; 15:1–32), the rich man and Lazarus (16:19–31), the persistent widow (18:1–8), and the Pharisee and the tax collector (18:9–14). All of these in some way carry the theme of *reversal*: humble "outsiders" receive blessings or commendation, while prideful "insiders" suffer rebuke or loss.

The journey climaxes with the episode of Zacchaeus (19:1–10). Zacchaeus is the ultimate of Israel's outcasts—not just a tax collector but a *chief* tax collector, the worst among the worst. Yet Jesus reaches out and offers salvation even to him. Luke 19:10 provides a fitting summary not only for the Zacchaeus account but for Luke's whole Gospel: "The Son of Man came to seek and to save the lost."

The journey to Jerusalem is also marked by Jesus' training of the disciples and by the theme of the cost of discipleship. In an opening passage, three people approach Jesus, all with aspirations of discipleship. For each, Jesus sets out the radical cost of following him (9:57–62). This is followed by many accounts about discipleship: the commissioning of the seventy (10:1–24), the unique revelation to the disciples through the Son (10:21–24), the story of Mary and Martha, in which Mary represents a true disciple (10:38–42), instruction on the cost of discipleship (14:25–35), the parable of the shrewd manager (16:1–13), and teaching on righteous living (prayer, 11:1–13; worry, 12:22–31; watchfulness, 12:35–48, 17:20–37; faith, 17:5–10; humility, 18:9–17; the dangers of wealth, 12:13–21, 16:19–31, 18:18–30).

Questions for Review and Discussion

1. What do we mean by the "literary unity" of Luke-Acts?
2. What is the purpose of Luke's Gospel?
3. What is the significance of the Nazareth sermon in Luke's Gospel? What is the significance of the travel narrative?

Recommended Resources

Bock, Darrell L. *Luke.* 2 vols. Baker Exegetical Commentary. Grand Rapids: Baker, 1994, 1996.

Green, Joel B. *The Gospel of Luke.* The New International Commentary on the New Testament. Grand Rapids: Eerdmans, 1997.

Strauss, Mark L. *Luke.* Zondervan Illustrated Bible Backgrounds Commentary, edited by Clinton Arnold. Grand Rapids: Zondervan, 2002.

CHAPTER 9

THEMES AND THEOLOGY OF LUKE'S GOSPEL

LUKE'S PORTRAIT OF JESUS: THE SAVIOR FOR ALL PEOPLE

Like a many-sided diamond, Luke's portrait of Jesus is multifaceted, and many titles are used for him. Since the overall theme of Luke-Acts is the arrival of God's end-times salvation (see the following), the best summarizing description for Jesus is *the Savior for all people*. Two titles that are especially important for Luke, helping to explain Jesus' saving role, are prophet and Christ (Messiah).

Prophet Like Moses, Mighty in Word and Deed. More than the other Gospels, Luke presents Jesus as a great prophet. When Jesus raises the widow's son from the dead, the people cry out, "A great prophet has appeared among us" (7:16). The disciples on the Emmaus road identify him as "a prophet, powerful in word and deed" (24:19). While the people link Jesus' prophetic office to his miracles and teaching, Jesus connects it especially to his suffering. At Nazareth, he affirms that "no prophet is accepted in his hometown" (4:24); later he accuses Israel of murdering her own prophets (11:47–52). As he journeys to Jerusalem, he affirms that "no prophet can die outside Jerusalem!" (13:33).

In Acts, this portrait is further clarified as Peter identifies Jesus as the prophet like Moses predicted in Deuteronomy 18:15 (Acts 3:22–23; cf. 7:37). Like Moses, Jesus proclaims God's word and performs miracles. And as Moses warned, those who do not heed God's prophet will be "completely cut off from their people" (3:23).

Luke's prophetic portrait thus has three key components: (1) Jesus performs miracles and proclaims God's word like the great prophets of old; (2) like the prophets, Jesus will suffer for his faithfulness; (3) if Israel does not heed God's prophet, divine judgment will follow. Luke's readers know that this will come to fulfillment in the destruction of Jerusalem.

Christ the Lord. Though Jesus' status as a prophet is important, it is exceeded by his role as Messiah. This is evident already in the birth narrative. While John the Baptist is a great prophet, Jesus is the Messiah and the Son of God (1:32–33). He is the "Savior . . . the Messiah, the Lord" (2:11). These four important titles—Messiah (Christ), Son of God, Savior, and Lord—are closely linked, all portraying Jesus as God's agent of deliverance, the fulfillment of God's saving purpose.

The startling revelation to which Luke's narrative builds is that God's salvation is accomplished not only through a suffering prophet but through the suffering Messiah. This is the main theme of the Emmaus resurrection account. Though the two disciples already recognize Jesus as a great prophet (24:19), Jesus opens their eyes to Scripture, showing them that *the Messiah had to suffer* (24:25–27). This is repeated to all of the disciples in the following episode (24:46) and serves as a repeated refrain in Acts (3:18; 17:3; 26:23). The Messiah fulfills the role of the Suffering Servant of Isaiah 53, bringing salvation to his people.

OTHER KEY THEMES AND THEOLOGY

Promise Fulfillment: The Salvation of God. The central theological theme of Luke-Acts is *the arrival of God's salvation, available now to people everywhere.* As predicted in the Prophets, God has acted through Jesus the Messiah to save his people Israel, and this salvation is now going forth to the whole world. Though the author slants his Gospel to a Gentile audience, he grounds it firmly in its Jewish roots. The key for Luke is the *continuity* between the history of Israel, the person and work of Jesus, and the establishment of the church.

While this theme reaches its climax in Acts, there are many examples of universality already in Luke's Gospel: the dating of Jesus' career in secular history (1:5; 2:1; 3:1–2), the genealogy descending all the way to Adam (3:23–38), the extended quote of Isaiah 40:3–5 ("all people will see God's salvation" [3:6]), and the reference to God's blessings for Gentiles in the Nazareth sermon (4:25–27). Various stories point forward to the Gentile mission. Jesus commends a centurion, saying, "I have not found such great faith even in Israel" (7:9). Though all of the Synoptics describe the mission of the Twelve (9:1–6), only Luke records a second mission involving seventy (or seventy-two) of his disciples (10:1–20). The number seventy probably represents the nations of the world, since seventy names are listed in the "table of nations" in Genesis 10. While the Hebrew text has seventy names, the Septuagint, the Greek Old Testament, lists seventy-two. This difference could account for the textual problem in Luke where some manuscripts read "seventy" and others "seventy-two" (vv. 1, 17). Luke (who generally follows the Septuagint) may have written "seventy-two" and later scribes altered his text to agree with the Hebrew text of Genesis 10.

This theme of universal salvation has both agreements and differences with Matthew. For Matthew, the commission to go to all nations is given only after Jesus' resurrection (Matt. 28:18–20; contrast Jesus' command in Matt. 10:5–6). In Luke, already in the birth narrative Simeon prophesies that salvation will extend to the Gentiles (2:32). All along it was God's plan to bring salvation to all peoples. By fulfilling the promises to Israel, Jesus becomes Savior of the whole world.

The Dawn of Salvation and the Coming of the Spirit. The theme of universal end-times salvation is closely linked by Luke to the coming of the Holy Spirit. In his Pentecost sermon in Acts, Peter cites the prophet Joel to show that "in the last days, God says, I will pour out my Spirit on all people" (Acts 2:17; Joel 2:28–32). A key theme for Luke is that *the coming of the Spirit heralds the dawn of the new age.*

The activity of the Spirit appears in three distinct periods in Luke-Acts. First, in Luke's birth narrative, the angel Gabriel prophesies that John will be filled with the Holy Spirit from his mother's womb (1:15; cf. 1:41–44), and Elizabeth and Zechariah are filled with the Spirit when they break into prophetic utterance (1:41, 67). The Spirit also rests on righteous Simeon, granting guidance and revelation (2:25–27). There was a widespread tradition in Judaism that the gift of prophecy had been withdrawn from Israel with the last of the prophets and would reappear in the end times. The renewal of the prophetic gift confirms that God's salvation is about to arrive.

Second, the Spirit also plays a prominent role in Jesus' ministry. In fulfillment of Isaiah's prophecies (42:1; 61:1–2), the Messiah is anointed by the Spirit at his baptism and filled with the Spirit to accomplish his task (Luke 3:22; 4:1, 14, 18; 10:21).

Third, following his ascension to God's right hand, Jesus pours out the Spirit (Acts 2:17–41) to empower his followers to accomplish their commission: taking the message of salvation to the ends of the earth. Jesus, endowed with God's Spirit during his earthly ministry, now mediates the Spirit to his church. Luke reveals a remarkably high Christology, as the Spirit of God becomes the Spirit of Jesus (Acts 16:6–7)—God's empowering presence among his people.

Divine Sovereignty and the Purpose of God. The theme of divine sovereignty permeates Luke's narrative. The Greek term *dei* ("it is necessary") occurs forty times in Luke-Acts, confirming that all that is happening is part of God's plan of salvation. While some scholars have linked this to the Greek conception of unchangeable fate, Luke speaks rather of God's purpose accomplished. Human free will is not obliterated; God works through human actions— both positive and negative—to achieve his purpose. Though wicked men put Jesus to death, this was God's plan, to accomplish salvation by raising him from the dead (Acts 2:23–24; cf. Luke 24:7, 26–27, 44–47; Acts 3:18; 4:28).

Salvation for Outsiders: A New Age of Reversals. This theme of reversal is an important one for Luke. Salvation comes not to the rich, powerful, and influential but to those who humble themselves before God. Jesus mingles with people from all positions in life—the poor, social outcasts, sinners, and tax collectors—offering salvation to all. This, in turn, serves as a preview of the Gentile mission in Acts, where the gospel will break out of its Jewish exclusiveness to become a message for all people everywhere.

(1) The Poor and Oppressed. In her birth narrative hymn, Mary praises God for exalting the humble and bringing down the mighty (1:51–53). In his inaugural sermon at Nazareth, Jesus preaches "good news to the poor" (4:16–22). Luke's Beatitudes are more concrete than Matthew's (6:20–21), and Luke balances these with woes against the

rich (6:24–25). Jesus tells parables of radical reversal of fortunes, like the rich fool (12:13–21) and the rich man and Lazarus (16:19–31).

(2) Sinners and Tax Collectors. The theme of Jesus' association with sinners—common in the Synoptics—is even more prevalent in Luke. Only Luke describes Jesus' anointing by an immoral woman who loves much because she has been forgiven much (7:36–50). Luke alone recounts the stories of Zacchaeus (19:1–10) and the repentant criminal on the cross (23:39–43). The parables of the prodigal son (15:11–32) and the Pharisee and the tax collector (18:9–14) are also unique to Luke. In all of these stories, it is not the religious but the repentant who find salvation.

(3) Samaritans. Luke speaks more of Samaritans than the other Gospels do. Jesus tells the parable of the good Samaritan (10:25–37), James and John are rebuked for wanting to call down fire from heaven on a Samaritan village (9:51–56), and the one leper who returns to thank Jesus is a Samaritan (17:11–19). This not only continues the theme of the gospel for the outcast (Samaritans were despised by Jews) but also sets the stage for Acts, in which the gospel will pass through Samaria on its way to the Gentile world (Acts 1:8; 8:4–25).

(4) Women. While women were generally relegated to positions of little status in the ancient world, Luke emphasizes the value Jesus placed on them as disciples and partners in ministry. No other Gospel gives so much emphasis to the women who played a part in Jesus' ministry. Luke refers to thirteen women not mentioned elsewhere in the Gospels. The first two chapters deal especially with women (Mary, Elizabeth, and Anna). Other passages include the widow of Nain (7:11–15), the woman who anointed Jesus' feet (7:36–50), the women who supported Jesus (8:1–3), the woman with a bleeding disorder (8:43–48), Mary and Martha (10:38–42), the "daughter of Abraham" (13:10–17), the poor widow (21:1–4), the "daughters of Jerusalem" who lamented Jesus (23:27–31), those who watched the crucifixion (23:49), and those who reported the resurrection (23:55–24:11).

Jerusalem and the Temple: Settings of Rejection and Salvation. Jerusalem plays a symbolic as well as geographical role in Luke-Acts. The Gospel begins and ends in the temple in Jerusalem (1:9; 24:53). Jerusalem is the place where God's presence dwells and from which his salvation will be achieved (9:31). Yet it is also a symbol of God's stubborn and rebellious people, and is where the prophets are murdered (13:33–34). The whole of Luke-Acts can be viewed symbolically as a journey to and from Jerusalem. Through much of the Gospel, Jesus journeys toward the city, arriving at the story's climax (9:51–56; 13:22, 33; 17:11; 18:31; 19:11, 28). He weeps over the city for her rejection of him and for the judgment which will follow (19:41–44). Yet through Jesus' death, resurrection, and ascension, salvation is achieved. The message of salvation now goes forth from Jerusalem to the ends of the earth (24:47; Acts 1:8).

Joy, Praise, and Celebration. The dawn of God's end-times salvation is marked by joy and praise to God. Words relating to joy, rejoicing, and praise are common throughout Luke-Acts. Gospel stories often end with the recipients of God's benefits praising God (5:25–26; 7:16; 13:13; 17:15, 18; 18:43). This theme continues in Acts (2:46–47), where praise accompanies both healings (3:8–9; 4:21) and the salvation of the Gentiles (11:18; 13:48; 21:19–20). Luke's message is clear: God is to be praised, for the joyful time of redemption has arrived.

Prayer and Intimate Fellowship with the Father. Luke lays special emphasis on Jesus' prayer life, referring to Jesus' prayers nine times (3:21; 5:16; 6:12; 9:18, 28; 11:1; 22:32; 23:34, 46). Jesus also teaches his disciples how to pray (11:1–4) and urges them to pray diligently during trials (18:1; 21:36; 22:40). Two of Luke's parables deal with the need for persistent prayer (11:5–13; 18:1–8). Luke's purpose in all of this is to show Jesus' unique relationship with God. To do his Father's will, Jesus must stay in intimate fellowship with him. The church of Luke's day would be encouraged to do the same.

READING LUKE TODAY

The generator chugs in the background as the young missionary, a wiry man with dark-rimmed glasses, shorts, and sandals, sets up the portable video machine. A white sheet hung between two trees serves as a screen. Around the glowing embers of a fire, thirty or so natives from the remote tribe sit on rocks and logs. As the video begins, they become mesmerized by the story unfolding before them. A child is born in poverty and grows to manhood. He begins an extraordinary career as a wandering teacher. The tribespeople nod and chatter among themselves as he tells parables and stories from everyday life. They watch in awe as he heals the sick, calms the raging sea, and raises the dead. Yet tragedy looms. The man is seized by his enemies, tortured, and hung on a wooden cross. He dies in agony and despair. The natives shout protests, sobbing and shouting as the tragedy plays out. But this is not the end. Their sorrow turns to joy as the man rises in victory from the dead. They cheer and weep as he ascends to heaven, announcing to his followers that salvation has been achieved.

Similar showings of this film have occurred countless times around the world, in remote jungle locations, in rural villages, and in teeming metropolises. In fact, it is the most widely viewed movie in human history. No, it is not *Star Wars* or *Titanic* but *The Jesus Film* produced by Campus Crusade for Christ (now known as Cru). It has been translated into more than seven hundred languages and has been seen by more than five billion people worldwide.

While movies about Jesus have traditionally drawn scenes from all four Gospels, *The Jesus Film* follows the narrative of one Gospel: Luke. It seems somehow appropriate that a film which has been dubbed into more languages and seen by more diverse people groups than any other is based on the Gospel which most clearly announces that salvation is for all people everywhere—from every tribe, nation, and language. I think Dr. Luke would be pleased.

Questions for Review and Discussion

1. Summarize Luke's portrait of Jesus. What two titles are especially important?
2. What is the central theological theme of Luke-Acts?
3. What role does the Holy Spirit play in Luke-Acts? What does Jerusalem symbolize?

Recommended Resources

Bock, Darrell L. *A Theology of Luke and Acts: God's Promised Program, Realized for All Nations.* Grand Rapids: Zondervan, 2012.

Green, Joel B. *The Theology of the Gospel of Luke.* Cambridge: Cambridge Univ. Press, 1995.

Marshall, I. Howard. *Luke: Historian and Theologian.* 3rd ed. Grand Rapids: Zondervan, 1998.

CHAPTER 10

INTRODUCING JOHN'S GOSPEL

The Gospel of John is unique among the Gospels. Though it is written in a simple style and with simple vocabulary, below this simplicity lies profound theological truth. As early as the third century, Clement of Alexandria was referring to this as a "spiritual Gospel." Paradoxically, new believers love John because even a child can understand it, while brilliant scholars continue to mine its depths for theological riches.

WHO WROTE JOHN'S GOSPEL?

Like the Synoptics, the fourth Gospel does not name its author. It comes close, however, by identifying the author as "the disciple whom Jesus loved": "This is the disciple who testifies to these things and who wrote them down. We know that his testimony is true" (21:20, 24).

This identification finds support in the narrative. The author claims to be an eyewitness (1:14; 19:35; 21:24, 25) and demonstrates firsthand knowledge of the events portrayed, often noting incidental details, like the number of years of illness ("thirty-eight" [5:5]), the name of the servant whose ear Peter sliced off ("Malchus" [18:10]), and the number of fish caught in Galilee ("153" [21:11]). The author shows good knowledge of Israel (4:3–4, 5), and particularly the city of Jerusalem (9:7; 10:23).

The author also has good knowledge of Jewish festivals and traditions (2:6, 23; 6:4; 7:2, 37–39; 10:22; 19:14, 31) and introduces Hebrew and Aramaic words like *Rabbi* and *Rabboni* ("Teacher," 1:38; 20:16), *Messias* ("Messiah," 1:41; 4:25), and *Kēphas* ("Rock," Peter,

1:42). While many scholars once believed that the fourth Gospel was the most Hellenistic (influenced by Greek thought) of the Gospels, today it is often viewed as the most Jewish. The discovery of the Dead Sea Scrolls, which reveal the same sort of dualism between light and darkness and between the children of God and the children of Satan, suggests that the traditions found in the fourth Gospel arose in a Palestinian context.

Who, then, was this Beloved Disciple? Some have suggested that he is a literary fiction representing the model of a faithful follower. This is unlikely, considering the explicit identification in 21:24. Others have pointed to Lazarus, since he first appears near the time the Beloved Disciple shows up (11:1; 13:23) and since he is explicitly said to be loved by Jesus (11:36). Most recently, Thomas has been suggested, since his story concludes the Gospel proper and since he asks to see Jesus' side (20:24–29; only the Beloved Disciple saw the spear-piercing, 19:34–35). The weight of evidence, however, favors the church's traditional identification of the Beloved Disciple as the apostle John, son of Zebedee and one of the Twelve. Irenaeus, writing in the late second century, claims that "afterwards, John, the disciple of the Lord, who also had leaned upon His breast, did himself publish a Gospel during his residence at Ephesus in Asia." Irenaeus says he received this tradition from Polycarp, a disciple of John himself.

This identification finds support in the narrative itself. The Beloved Disciple appears as a close associate of Peter (13:24; 20:2–10; 21:2, 7, 20–24), suggesting he was one of the inner circle of disciples (Peter, James, and John). Since James was martyred at an early date (Acts 12:1–5), the apostle John remains the most likely candidate.

WHERE AND WHEN WAS JOHN'S GOSPEL WRITTEN?

Since the eighteenth century, it was common among critical scholars to date the fourth Gospel to the late second century, assuming its exalted view of Christ was a late development in the church. The discovery of the John Rylands manuscript (P^{52}), a small fragment of John dated to the first half of the second century, has refuted this claim. Most scholars today date the Gospel to the late first century.

Church tradition claims that the apostle John ministered in Ephesus in his later life and that it was there he wrote the Gospel. While such traditions are not infallible, this setting fits well the Gospel's content. Ephesus was a major crossroads of the Roman world and had a large Jewish population. In the late first century, Christians had broken with the Jewish synagogue and were increasingly viewed with suspicion by the secular authorities. This alienation would account for the Gospel's strong polemic against both the "Jews" and the "world."

WHY WAS JOHN'S GOSPEL WRITTEN?

The fourth Gospel states its purpose clearly: "Jesus performed many other signs in the presence of his disciples, which are not recorded in this book. But these are written that you may believe that Jesus is the Messiah, the Son of God, and that by believing you may have life in his name" (John 20:30–31).

The author writes to call forth faith in Jesus. While this suggests an evangelistic purpose, the Gospel seems intended to bring confidence for believers as well. The reading "that you might believe" (*hina pisteusēte*, an aorist subjunctive) is disputed, and some early manuscripts could be translated "that you might continue to believe" (*hina pisteuēte*, a present subjunctive). These two purposes—to provoke belief and perseverance—are not mutually exclusive, and both are probably aspects of the author's purpose. The bottom line is that John's Gospel is a call to decision. Readers are not only introduced to the story of Jesus Christ, the Son of God; they are called to respond in faith to him.

LITERARY FEATURES OF JOHN'S GOSPEL

Unique Content. The reader approaching John's Gospel immediately notices a picture strikingly different from that in the Synoptic Gospels. While the Synoptics share many common features, about 90 percent of John is unique. Key features of Jesus' ministry are absent. There are no exorcisms or parables (but see 12:24), no table fellowship with sinners. The key Synoptic phrase "kingdom of God" occurs only twice. Most of Jesus' teaching is unique, and five of John's eight miracles do not occur in the Synoptics. Many key Synoptic events are absent, including Jesus' baptism, his temptation, the transfiguration, and the institution of the Lord's Supper.

John also includes many stories not found in the Synoptics: the miracle of changing water to wine, Jesus' conversations with Nicodemus and the Samaritan woman, the raising of Lazarus, Jesus' washing of the disciples' feet, the High Priestly Prayer, the account of doubting Thomas, and many others.

Only John reports Jesus' extensive Judean ministry, as he travels back and forth between Galilee and Judea. The Synoptics are more linear, with a single movement from Galilee to Jerusalem. They provide little information concerning the length of Jesus' ministry, mentioning only the Passover associated with Jesus' crucifixion. John refers to three Passovers (2:13; 6:4; 11:55) and possibly a fourth (5:1), suggesting a ministry between two and a half and three and a half years long.

Jesus also speaks more openly about himself in John than in the other Gospels. In the Synoptics, Jesus' teaching focuses on the kingdom of God and his role as its inaugurator. In John, he speaks much more about himself and his unique relationship to the Father. Jesus makes seven "I am" statements—metaphorical descriptions of himself and his role as the Son who reveals the Father.

Unique Literary Style. John's literary style is also unique. It is characterized by simplicity, with short sentences connected by coordinate conjunctions ("and"). The style is repetitious, with parallelism used for emphasis (John 14:27: "Peace I leave with you; my peace I give you"). There are also many contrasts: light and darkness, truth and falsehood, life and death, above and below. While John's vocabulary is basic, seemingly "simple" words like *know, abide, believe, witness, truth, life, light, glory,* and *the world* carry profound theological significance.

This unique style relates not only to the narrator's comments but also to Jesus' words. Jesus speaks not in parables and short wisdom sayings, as in the Synoptics, but in long discourses and dialogues with his opponents. The Synoptics relate Jesus' teaching on the kingdom of God, repentance, and right behavior toward God and others.

In John, Jesus speaks more on philosophical issues of truth, life, and knowing God. Jesus' style of speaking so resembles the narrator's that sometimes it is difficult to tell when Jesus stops speaking and the narrator starts. For example, in Jesus' dialogue with Nicodemus in John 3, most "red letter" Bibles continue Jesus' words through verse 21. But it is not clear in the text whether he is still speaking. Jesus speaks in the first person ("I") in verses 3–12, then switches to the third person with reference to the "Son of Man" in verses 13–15. Verses 16–21 continue in the third person but now speak of Jesus as the "Son" sent by the Father. Are these Jesus' words or John's? It is difficult to tell.

This raises the difficult issue of how much this Gospel records the actual words of Jesus and how much of it is the author's interpretation of Jesus' life and teaching. This question does not challenge the authority of the text, since inspiration applies to everything the author wrote—speech, actions, narration, interpretation. But it does affect how we view the literary genre of the fourth Gospel. Is this Gospel meant to be a historical record of Jesus' life or a theological meditation on its significance? Or both?

The Relationship of John to the Synoptics. The many differences between John and the Synoptics also raise the question of their literary relationship. Did the author of the fourth Gospel know and use the Synoptics, or is he writing independently of them? Until the twentieth century, it was generally believed that John wrote to supplement the other Gospels. The tide turned in the mid-twentieth century, when P. Gardner-Smith and others argued for John's literary independence. Today scholars are divided. A minority still hold to John's direct dependence on the Synoptics. Others, like Gardner-Smith, reject any link apart from the use of common traditions. A mediating position denies direct borrowing but thinks John knows one or more of the Synoptics and assumes his readers will be familiar with their content. This third perspective is perhaps the most appealing, since it recognizes both John's dependence and his independence. He is interacting within the world of early Christianity yet writes to accomplish his own unique purpose.

John's Structure. The Gospel has a relatively simple structure. It begins with a magnificent prologue, perhaps the greatest statement concerning the identity and incarnation of Jesus ever written (1:1–18). The prologue identifies Jesus as the preexistent "Word" *(Logos)*— God's self-revelation—who became a human being to bring light and grace and truth to humankind.

The main body of the Gospel has two parts, sometimes called the Book of Signs (1:19–12:50) and the Book of Glory (13:1–20:31). The former contains seven miracles, or "signs," that reveal Jesus' identity and call people to faith in him. The Book of Glory is so called because Jesus' death and resurrection is repeatedly described as his glorification (7:39; 12:23; 13:31–32; 17:1, 4; cf. 21:19). This section contains the Last Supper, during which Jesus washes the disciples' feet (chap. 13), the Farewell Discourse, when he promises the Holy Spirit to teach and guide them (chaps. 14–16), Jesus' prayer for his disciples (chap. 17), and the passion (chaps. 18–19) and resurrection (chap. 20) narratives.

The book ends with an epilogue (chap. 21) describing a postresurrection appearance to the disciples, Jesus' commissioning of Peter to "feed my sheep," and the identification of the Beloved Disciple as the author.

Teaching Types. Jesus' teaching in John's Gospel falls into three types: interviews with individuals (chaps. 3–4), dialogue and debates with the Jewish religious leaders (chaps. 5–12), and private teaching of his disciples (chaps. 13–17).

(1) Personal Interviews. Twice John describes Jesus' extended conversations with individuals: with Nicodemus and the Samaritan woman. Both follow a similar pattern: Jesus introduces a spiritual metaphor (new birth, 3:3; living water, 4:7, 10) which provokes interest but also misunderstanding (3:4; 4:9, 11). Jesus clarifies the spiritual significance (3:5; 4:13–14, 21–24). The episodes climax as Jesus identifies himself (3:13–21; 4:25–26), an implicit call to faith.

(2) Public Debate. The main part of the Gospel contains extended dialogue and debate between Jesus and his opponents. These debates, too, follow a similar pattern. Jesus performs a miracle or teaches. This provokes a response or challenge from his hearers, followed by further teaching from Jesus. This to-and-fro eventually concludes with a response toward Jesus—often mixed—from the hearers. The debate in chapter 7 ends with some claiming that Jesus

is "the prophet," others that he is the Messiah, and still others denying that the Messiah could come from Galilee. The narrator concludes, "Thus the people were divided because of Jesus" (7:43).

(3) Private Teaching. The Last Supper and Jesus' Farewell Discourse (chaps. 13–17) make up the third type of extended teaching. Jesus describes the coming role of the Holy Spirit, identifies himself as the true vine in whom the disciples must abide, instructs them on aspects of community life, and warns them of coming persecution. The message throughout is encouragement to faithfulness and assurance of his abiding presence. In chapter 17, sometimes called the High Priestly Prayer, Jesus prays that the disciples be kept safe and remain faithful.

The "Signs" of the Gospel. While the Gospel records only eight of Jesus' miracles, these "signs" *(sēmeia)* play a key role in Jesus' self-revelation. Seven appear in the Gospel proper, and one (the miraculous catch of fish) in the epilogue.

1. Changing water into wine (2:1–11)
2. Healing an official's son (4:43–54)
3. Healing a disabled man at the Bethesda pool (5:1–15)
4. Feeding the five thousand (6:1–14)
5. Walking on water (6:16–21)
6. Healing a man born blind (9:1–12)
7. Raising Lazarus (11:1–44)
8. Causing a miraculous catch of fish (21:1–14)

The signs are often interpreted by Jesus' teaching. For example, Jesus feeds the five thousand and then gives a discourse on the bread of life (chap. 6). Similarly, he raises Lazarus from the dead after identifying himself as the resurrection and the life (11:25–26).

Each sign reveals Jesus' identity and mission and calls forth a decision from the hearers. After the first sign, changing water to wine at the wedding in Cana, the narrator notes that "what Jesus did here in Cana of Galilee was the first of the signs through which he revealed his glory; and his disciples believed in him" (2:11). The sign reveals Jesus' glory, which provokes faith in him as the self-revelation of God. This is somewhat different from the Synoptic miracles, which point to the in-breaking power of the kingdom of God and to Jesus' authority as its inaugurator (Matt. 12:28; Luke 11:20). The raising of Lazarus is the climax and the greatest of the seven Gospel signs, serving as a preview for the ultimate event to which this sign points—Jesus' own resurrection. It also carries the plot forward, both by provoking faith in Jesus (11:45, 48; 12:11) and by prompting the religious leaders to act decisively against him (11:48–51).

Questions for Review and Discussion

1. What was John's purpose in writing his Gospel?
2. In what ways is John's Gospel unique among the four?
3. Describe the two parts of the main structure of John's Gospel. What role do the signs play?

Recommended Resources

Burge, Gary M. *John.* NIV Application Commentary. Grand Rapids: Zondervan, 2000.

Carson, D. A. *The Gospel according to John.* Pillar New Testament Commentary. Grand Rapids: Eerdmans, 1991.

Köstenberger, Andreas. *John.* Baker Exegetical Commentary on the New Testament. Grand Rapids: Baker, 2004.

CHAPTER 11

THEMES AND THEOLOGY OF JOHN'S GOSPEL

JOHN'S PORTRAIT OF JESUS: THE SON WHO REVEALS THE FATHER

Jesus' identity is on center stage throughout the fourth Gospel, which presents the most exalted Christology in the New Testament. Jesus is the unique Son of God who has come from the Father. He is God's Word *(Logos)*, his self-revelation (1:1, 14, 18). Whoever has seen him has seen the Father (14:9). While distinct from the Father ("with God," 1:1), he is fully God ("was God," 1:1; 20:28), the "I AM" who existed before Abraham (8:24, 28, 58; cf. Ex. 3:13–14). He shares God's attributes. He is the creator of all things (1:3, 10), the giver and sustainer of life (5:16–18, 26; 6:27, 35, 50–58), who will raise the dead (5:21, 25; 4:53; 6:39–40, 44, 54; 10:28; 11:25–26) and serve as final judge (5:22, 27). He is omniscient (1:48; 2:24–25; 6:15; 8:14; 13:1, 11; 21:17). As the Son sent from above, he provides the only access to the Father and to eternal life: "No one comes to the Father except through me" (14:6; cf. 3:16, 36; 4:14; 5:21–26; 6:33, 35, 51–58, 68; 8:12; 10:10, 17–18; 11:25; 17:2–3). The Father and Son operate in complete unity (10:30; 14:10) and know one another perfectly (10:15).

While the Gospel speaks of Jesus as equal with God (5:18, sometimes called ontological equality), there is also a strong functional subordination. By this we mean that while Jesus is fully divine, he lives in complete dependence on the Father. The Son does nothing by himself but only what the Father directs him to do (5:19; 8:29). He has come to do the will of the Father who sent him (3:16, 34; 4:34; 6:38; 7:28; 8:26,

42; 12:49) and to bring glory to him (11:4; 14:13; 17:4). This functional subordination is in line with the central theme of the Gospel: *the role of the Son is to reveal the Father and bring others into a relationship with him.*

While John's exalted Christology exceeds traditional Jewish expectations for the Messiah, the author does not avoid messianic categories. As in the Synoptics, Jesus is the Messiah (John 1:41; 4:25–26), the king of Israel (1:49; 12:13), and the fulfillment of Old Testament prophecies. In some ways, John has a stronger Jewish accent than the other Gospels, charting Jesus' ministry according to Jewish festivals and building images and allusions that echo Old Testament themes. Only John uses the transliterated form *messias*, from the Hebrew *mashiach* ("Messiah" = "Anointed One," 1:41; 4:25). Elsewhere in the New Testament (and nineteen times in John), the Greek translation *christos* is used ("Christ" = "Anointed One"). The author is clearly concerned to show that the community that worships Jesus the Messiah is the true people of God, the heirs of the promises made to Israel.

OTHER KEY THEMES

The Revelation of the Father through the Son. As noted previously, the central theme of the Gospel is the revelation of the Father through the Son. God loved the world so much that he sent his Son to save it. Those who believe in the Son have eternal life. Those who reject him are condemned already (3:16–18). As God's "Word" made flesh, Jesus has perfect knowledge of the Father and now offers this knowledge and relationship to all who believe. Images of light, life, and sight characterize those who come to know the Father through Jesus the Son.

Over against the themes of knowledge and sight are Jesus' opponents, who remain in darkness and are blind to the truth. The themes of misunderstanding and spiritual blindness permeate the Gospel. Jesus' opponents are ignorant of spiritual realities because they do not know the Father or the Son (7:28; 8:19, 55; 15:21; 17:25).

Salvation as Knowing God, Eternal Life in the Present. In the Synoptic Gospels, salvation is identified especially with entrance into the kingdom of God. In John, it is usually described as eternal life. John does occasionally speak of the kingdom of God (see John 3:3, 5), and the Synoptics of eternal life (see Mark 10:17, 30 par.), but these references are exceptional. Both John and the Synoptics describe salvation as both already and not yet, having both present and future dimensions. For future eschatology in John, see 3:16; 6:39; 10:28; 14:3, 28; 21:23. But the greater emphasis in the fourth Gospel is on the present. The Son came to bring eternal life, and this is now available to all who believe (5:24–26). Jesus says, "I have come that they may have life, and have it to the full" (10:10). While Jesus will raise the dead on the last day (6:39, 40, 44, 54), he is already the resurrection and the life, bestowing eternal life on those who believe (11:25). This is called "realized eschatology"; God's end-times salvation is already present in the life of the believer.

Salvation is a present possession because eternal life is equivalent to *knowing God*, a relationship with the Father through the Son. "Now this is eternal life: that they know you, the only true God, and Jesus Christ, whom you have sent" (17:3). This relationship with God happens through regeneration, being "born again" (3:3), when the Father and the Son come to live in the believer (14:23). When this happens, they come to know the truth and are set free (8:32, 36). They now walk in the light (3:21; 8:12; 12:36, 46).

The Paraclete. Since the Son brings life and light, how will the disciples manage after he leaves? The answer is that he will send another "counselor" or "advocate" *(paraklētos)*, the Holy Spirit, who will mediate his presence to them. The role of the Spirit is developed in Jesus' Farewell Discourse (chaps. 14–16). Jesus here describes his soon departure and promises to send the Spirit to take his place. The Spirit will mediate the presence of the Father and the Son to the disciples, teaching, guiding, and comforting them (14:16–20, 26–27; 15:26–27; 16:5–16). It is in fact better that he is leaving, since the indwelling presence of the Father and the Son will enable them to do even greater works than his (14:12; 16:7).

But the disciples can be successful only if they abide in him. Just as a branch gains sustenance from the vine, so they will bear fruit only by staying close to him (15:1–8). Abiding in Jesus is essential because of the hostile environment in which the disciples will live. The world alienated from the Father and the Son will hate and persecute them, throwing them out of the synagogues and even killing them (15:18–16:4). Yet the Spirit has a role with reference to the world as well, convicting it of sin, righteousness, and judgment (16:5–11). Like a prosecuting attorney, the Spirit will reveal the guilt and coming judgment of the world. To the disciples, however, the Spirit will reveal all truth (16:12–15). This probably refers not only to the apostles' writing of Scripture but also to divine guidance for all believers.

John shares with Luke-Acts a special interest in the work of the Spirit. In both, the Spirit represents the continuing presence of Jesus in his church, empowering, guiding, and directing the disciples on their mission. Yet there are important differences. For Luke, the coming of the Spirit is especially the fulfillment of prophecy, the evidence of the dawning of the new age of salvation and proof that the last days have begun (Acts 2). In John, the greater emphasis is on the Spirit's role as *another* paraclete, who will act in Jesus' place to mediate the presence of the Father. As Jesus imparted life, light, and knowledge of the Father to the disciples, so now the Spirit will do the same thing. He will guide them into all truth, testifying about Jesus and reminding them of all he taught them (14:26; 15:26).

Johannine Dualism. John's theology has a strong dualistic bent. By dualism we do not mean a distinction between the material world and the spirit world, as in Platonic or Gnostic dualism. Johannine dualism, rather, represents a strict dichotomy between those on the side of Jesus and those opposed to him. This is the difference between good and evil, light and darkness, the children of God and the children of the devil. There is little gray or middle ground. You are either for God or for Satan, of light or of darkness, from above or from below.

John's theological dualism is particularly evident in his portrayal of Jesus' opponents. These are the religious leaders, the world, and Satan. The Greek term *Ioudaioi* ("Jews," "Judeans," or "Jewish leaders") occurs only rarely in the Synoptics but appears sixty-three times in John. While occasionally carrying a neutral sense of ethnic descent (2:6; 4:9), it is usually negative, referring to the Jewish religious leaders who oppose Jesus. The best explanation of this terminology is that John is writing at a time when the church has broken with the synagogue. The debate between Jewish Christianity and Judaism is no longer an inter-Jewish debate but one between Christians and Jews.

John's portrayal of the Jewish religious leaders is not wholly negative. While most reject Jesus, others believe (2:23; 7:31; 8:31; 11:45;

12:42), and the narrator often refers to their divisions (7:12, 43; 9:16; 10:19). Yet as the narrative progresses, hostility increases as they resolve to kill Jesus (5:18; 7:1, 19, 25; 8:37, 40; 10:31; 11:53). They do not believe their own Scriptures, which testify to him (5:39, 47), and so God's word does not dwell in them (5:38). They do not know the Father or the Son (8:19, 47, 55). They are "of this world" (8:23) and "from below" (8:23). Judas, who himself is called "a devil" (6:70), is prompted by Satan to betray Jesus into the hands of the religious leaders (13:2, 27), who are themselves children of the devil (8:44).

These connections between the religious leaders, the world, and Satan reflect John's dualistic perspective. By opposing Jesus, these leaders have allied themselves with the evil world system (1:10; 7:7; 14:17, 22) and with Satan, "the prince of this world" (12:31; 14:30; 16:11). The "world" *(kosmos),* like the *Ioudaioi,* can be used neutrally of the place where people dwell (1:10; 9:39; 13:1; 16:21, 28; 17:5, 24; 18:37) or the people whom God sent Jesus to save (1:10; 3:16, 17; 4:42; 6:33, 51; 8:12; 9:5; 17:21). More often, it carries connotations of the evil world system ruled by Satan (1:10; 7:7; 12:31; 14:17, 22, 30; 15:18–19; 16:8, 11, 20, 33; 17:16). Like the religious leaders, the world does not know Jesus (1:10; 17:25) and so hates him (7:7; 15:18) and his followers (17:14).

Metaphor and Symbol. John's "spiritual" Gospel often operates at the level of metaphor and symbol. Jesus is identified at the outset as the "Word," a metaphor for God's communicative presence. John the Baptist calls him the "Lamb of God," a symbol for sacrificial death (1:29, 36). The seven "I am" statements are metaphorical. Jesus is the bread of life (6:35), the light of the world (8:12; 9:5), the door or gate for the sheep (10:7), the good shepherd (10:11, 14), the resurrection and the life (11:25), the one true path to life (14:6), and the true vine (15:1). Like so much else in this Gospel, simple and everyday images reveal profound theological truth.

For those without faith, however, the symbols mask the truth, creating confusion and misunderstanding. Nicodemus cannot comprehend the metaphor of new birth. The woman at the well is at first confused by Jesus' reference to living water. His Jewish opponents are baffled when Jesus—referring to his own body—says, "Destroy this temple, and I will raise it again in three days" (2:19). Like the

Synoptic parables, the metaphors and symbols of the fourth Gospel both reveal and conceal (cf. Mark 4:11–12).

Irony. Since misunderstanding is a common theme in John, irony plays a major role as characters deny or question things that, ironically, are true. Nathanael asks if anything good can come from Nazareth (1:46). The Samaritan woman asks Jesus sarcastically, "Are you greater than our father Jacob?" (4:12). The religious leaders reject Jesus since they know he came from Galilee and the Messiah's origin is supposed to be unknown (7:27). But in fact they do not know where he is from, since his true origin is from heaven (3:13, 31; 6:32–33, 38, 50–51). Similar irony pervades the account of the healing of the man born blind (chap. 9). As the man progressively gains greater spiritual in*sight*, the religious leaders decline toward greater blindness. The man first identifies Jesus as "the man they call Jesus" (v. 11), then "a prophet" (v. 17), then "from God" (v. 33), and finally worships him with the confession "Lord, I believe" (v. 38). The religious leaders are at first divided about Jesus (v. 16), then call him "a sinner" (v. 24). Johannine irony climaxes the encounter as they ask sarcastically, "What? Are we blind too?" (v. 40). In fact they are!

Irony also appears in double meanings given to words. Jesus tells Nicodemus that he must be born again (3:3). The Greek *anōthen* can mean either "again" or "from above." While Nicodemus misunderstands this as physical rebirth, Jesus means spiritual or heavenly birth through the Spirit. Jesus offers the Samaritan woman living water (4:10). She misunderstands this to mean fresh spring water, but Jesus means spiritual water which gives eternal life (4:13–14).

In a greater sense, the whole Gospel is ironic, since God's great salvation is accomplished through the death of his Son. In a play on words, Jesus repeatedly refers to his crucifixion as a "lifting up" (3:14; 8:28; 12:32–34). The physical lifting of the cross—a symbol of horrific death—points to Jesus' glorious victory and exaltation following his resurrection.

READING JOHN TODAY

With its elegant simplicity and deep spiritual insight, John's Gospel is perhaps the most loved of the four Gospels. It is also the most widely distributed, sometimes being printed as a separate pamphlet, an evangelistic tract to lead people to Christ. I have one of these on my shelf with an introduction in many different languages and a conclusion explaining how to receive Jesus as Savior. The author of the fourth Gospel would surely be pleased with such a publication, fitting as it does his narrative purpose: "that you may believe that Jesus is the Messiah, the Son of God, and that by believing you may have life in his name" (20:31). John's Gospel is fundamentally a call to decision. Like the characters in the story—Nicodemus, the Samaritan woman, Peter, and others—each reader encounters the claims of Jesus and must respond with acceptance or rejection.

Nor is there any middle ground in this decision. Though a beautiful literary work, John's Gospel does not espouse a spiritual sentimentality or religious pluralism. John draws a stark contrast between those who believe in Jesus and those who reject him, the children of God and the children of Satan, those in the light and those in darkness. Jesus preaches an exclusive gospel: the Son is the only way to the Father. All others stand condemned. Forged in the heat of competing religious claims, the Gospel is both a call for faith leading to life and a warning against disbelief leading to death. To be sure, this is an unpopular message in today's society, in which claims to absolute truth are dismissed as naive and relativism is the order of the day. But it is a message the fourth Evangelist passionately believed the world needed to hear.

Questions for Review and Discussion

1. In what way is John's Christology unique? What are its main themes?
2. How is salvation portrayed in John's Gospel?
3. What do we mean by Johannine dualism?

Recommended Resources

Beasley-Murray, George R. *Gospel of Life: Theology in the Fourth Gospel.* Peabody, MA: Hendrickson, 1991.

Köstenberger, Andreas. *A Theology of John's Gospel and Letters: The Word, the Christ, the Son of God.* Biblical Theology of the New Testament Series. Grand Rapids: Zondervan, 2009.

Smith, D. Moody. *The Theology of the Gospel of John.* Cambridge: Cambridge Univ. Press, 1995.

CHAPTER 12

THE HISTORICAL RELIABILITY OF THE GOSPELS

Christians are often surprised to learn that many biblical scholars reject the notion that Jesus was anything more than a mere man. How can this be, they ask, if Jesus himself claimed to be the Son of God and even God himself? Were not the Gospels written by eyewitnesses or close associates of the eyewitnesses?

The answer is that many critical scholars do not consider the Gospels to be eyewitness accounts. They assume rather that the Gospels are the result of a long process of creative storytelling and mythmaking by communities far removed from the historical Jesus.

In the end, one's assessment of the historical Jesus depends on the reliability attributed to the Gospels. Those who take the Gospels as generally reliable come up with a Jesus very much like the one portrayed in the Gospels. Those who doubt their reliability come up with a very different Jesus. In this chapter, we turn to the question of the historical reliability of the Gospels.

WERE THE GOSPEL WRITERS BIASED?

A common accusation against the Gospels is that the beliefs of the Evangelists distorted their presentation of Jesus. Were the Gospel writers biased? If we mean by biased "holding certain convictions," then the answer is of course yes, since there is no such thing as an unbiased historian. Everyone has a worldview and a belief system through which they process reality. The Gospel writers passionately believed in the message they proclaimed, and desired others to believe it. Did this distort their conclusions? An analogy is appropriate here. Some of the most important accounts of the Nazi Holocaust were composed by Jews. Does this fact render the accounts inaccurate? On the contrary, those passionately interested in the events are often the most meticulous in recording them. To claim that the Gospels cannot be historical because they were written by believers is fallacious. The important question is not whether the Gospel writers were biased but whether they were reliable historians.

LUKE-ACTS AND ANCIENT HISTORY WRITING

Did the Gospel writers write accurate history? As we have seen, Luke indicates this was his intent: "Many have undertaken to draw up an account of the things that have been fulfilled among us, just as they were handed down to us by those who from the first were eyewitnesses and servants of the word. With this in mind, since I myself have carefully investigated everything from the beginning, I too decided to write an orderly account for you, most excellent Theophilus, so that you may know the certainty of the things you have been taught" (Luke 1:1–4).

Notice the piling up of historical terms: "eyewitnesses," "carefully investigated," "orderly account," "certainty." Luke clearly claims to be writing accurate history. Some critics respond that these claims are of little value, since history writing in a modern sense was unknown in the ancient world. While it is certainly true that some ancient historians were better than others, it is wrong to deny that good history existed in the ancient world. The Hellenistic historian Polybius criticizes other writers for making up dramatic scenes and calls on them to "simply record what really happened and what really was said" (*Histories* 2.56.10). This shows not only that there were good and bad historians but that intelligent writers and readers in the first century distinguished fact from fiction. Luke's reliability as a historian must be judged from the evidence, not from sweeping generalizations about ancient history.

So was Luke a reliable historian? In *The Book of Acts in the Setting of Hellenistic History*, Colin Hemer conducted a detailed critical study of Luke's historical references in Acts, concluding that Luke was a meticulous and reliable historian. Particularly striking is Luke's attention to historical detail, providing names of cities and titles of government officials that are accurate for both time and place. This is especially significant since such names changed frequently. For example, Luke accurately identifies Sergius Paulus as *anthypatos* ("proconsul") of Cyprus (Acts 13:7) and Publius as the *prōtos* (chief official) of Malta (Acts 28:7). City officials are *stratēgoi* in Philippi (Acts 16:20), *politarchai* in Thessalonica (Acts 17:6), and *asiarchai* in Ephesus (Acts 19:31)—all historically accurate designations. This would be like someone accurately distinguishing titles like supervisor, councilor, mayor, governor, senator, representative, speaker of the house, vice president, and president. We would expect those who knew the meaning of such titles to have firsthand knowledge of American government. If Luke was so meticulous with these kinds of details in Acts, he was likely also careful in research and writing about the Jesus tradition.

A GENERALLY RELIABLE GOSPEL TRADITION

We may speak of Luke's value as a historian, but were the traditions he received reliable? We turn next to some evidence that the church carefully passed down the traditions about Jesus.

The Testimony of the Eyewitnesses. Some critics claim that the eyewitnesses to the events of Jesus had little to do with passing down the tradition. But this contradicts the strong evidence that the apostles were the primary guardians and transmitters of the story of Jesus (Luke 1:2; Acts 1:21–22; 2:42; 6:2, 4; 1 Cor. 9:1; Gal. 2:2–10). Throughout the New Testament, the testimony of eyewitnesses is highly esteemed (John 19:35; 21:24; Acts 1:21–22; 10:39, 41; 1 Cor. 15:6; 1 Peter 5:1; 2 Peter 1:16; 1 John 1:1–3).

The Church's Willingness to Preserve Difficult Sayings. Further evidence of the church's accurate transmission is their faithfulness in preserving difficult sayings of Jesus. For example, in Mark 13:32, Jesus admits that even he doesn't know the day or the hour of his return. It seems unlikely that the church would create a saying that attributed ignorance to Jesus. If stories and sayings were constantly being created and altered, why not simply eliminate those that presented theological difficulties? (See also Matt. 10:5–6; Mark 9:1.)

The Absence of Discussion on Key Issues in the Later Church. If the later church created words of Jesus to meet its present needs, why are there no sayings for many topics that were burning issues in the early church? There is nothing about circumcision and the charismatic gifts, and very little on baptism, the Gentile mission, food laws, and church-state relations.

The Ethical Argument: Were the Disciples Deceivers? But did the eyewitnesses tell the truth? Or were the disciples deceivers who propagated a great fraud in order to keep the Jesus story alive? It pushes the limits of credulity to argue that the same Christians who taught the greatest ethical system in the world, passionately proclaimed the truth of their message, and suffered and died for their faith were also dishonest schemers and propagators of a great fraud.

These points suggest, at the least, the general reliability of the Gospel tradition. The church seems to have taken special care in accurately passing down Jesus' words and deeds.

CONTRADICTIONS BETWEEN THE GOSPELS?

With so much common material in the Gospels, it is not surprising that there are apparent contradictions between them. How do we account for these? In reality, most claims of contradictions result from demanding more historical precision than the authors intended to provide. The Gospels were never meant to be videotapes of events or word-for-word transcripts. It is the normal method of history writing—both ancient and modern—to summarize accounts, paraphrase speeches, omit extraneous details, and report events from a particular vantage point. Most supposed contradictions in the Gospels can be readily explained from common practices in history writing.

Paraphrasing and Interpretation. New Testament scholars have long recognized that in most cases we have not the *exact words (ipsissima verba)* of Jesus but rather his *authentic voice (ipsissima vox).* The essential meaning is communicated using different words. In one sense this is obvious, since Jesus normally spoke Aramaic but the

Gospels are in Greek. Many differences in wording or idiom may be attributed to differences in translation and style.

As authoritative interpreters, the Gospel writers sometimes move beyond simple translation or paraphrase to bring out the theological significance of Jesus' words. For example, Jesus' beatitude in Luke "blessed are you who are poor" (Luke 6:20) becomes in Matthew "blessed are the poor in spirit" (Matt. 5:3). While it is possible that Matthew's phrase is original or that Jesus said both on different occasions, more likely Matthew is clarifying the spiritual significance of Jesus' words.

Another example is the centurion's statement from the foot of the cross. While in Matthew and Mark, the centurion says, "Surely this man was *the Son of God!*" (Mark 15:39; Matt. 27:54; emphasis added), in Luke he says, "Surely this was a *righteous* [or 'innocent'] man" (Luke 23:47, emphasis added). Both statements are important climaxes in their respective Gospels. Son of God is a key title for both Matthew and Mark, and Jesus' innocence is a major theme in Luke's passion narrative. The centurion may have said both, or Luke may be emphasizing that Jesus' status as Son of God means he is the innocent and righteous Servant of the LORD (Isa. 53:11). He would thus be citing not the exact words but the theological implication of the centurion's statement.

The point is that we cannot always be sure what is verbatim citation and what is the author's authoritative explanation. But to label these as errors or contradictions is to treat the Gospels as something they were never intended to be.

Abbreviation and Omission. The Gospel writers are clearly selective, omitting many extraneous details and including features important to their narrative purposes. Sometimes abbreviation or omission leaves readers with the impression of contradiction.

Matthew is famous for abbreviating accounts. While in Mark, Jesus curses the fig tree on one day and the disciples discover it withered the next, in Matthew the cursing and withering appear together (Mark 11:12–14, 20–25; Matt. 21:18–22). We may conclude that Matthew is interested not in providing a strict chronology but rather in emphasizing the miracle. Similarly, the raising of Jairus's daughter is greatly abbreviated in Matthew, leaving the incorrect impression that the daughter was already dead when Jairus first spoke with Jesus (Matt. 9:18–26; Mark 5:21–43; Luke 8:40–56).

Reordering of Events and Sayings. As we have seen, the Gospel writers do not necessarily follow a chronological order and often rearrange events for topical or theological reasons. A classic example is the temptation account in Matthew and Luke, where the last two temptations are in reverse order (Matt. 4:1–11; Luke 4:1–13). It is difficult to tell which is original, since both climax at locations appropriate to their respective Gospels. Luke, who stresses the importance of Jerusalem and the temple, ends with Jesus on the pinnacle of the temple. Matthew, who portrays mountains as places of revelation, ends with Jesus on a high mountain. Whichever is original, the changed order does not negate the historicity of the event.

Reporting Similar Events and Sayings. Related to reordering is the question of similar events or sayings. Did Jesus clear the temple once or twice? While the Synoptic Gospels place the event at the end of Jesus' ministry (Matt. 21:12–13; Mark 11:15–17; Luke 19:45–46), John places it at the beginning (John 2:13–17). It is not far-fetched to think that after three years Jesus would have lashed out again at the marketplace atmosphere of the temple. On the other hand, it was also within the Evangelists' authority to rearrange events to emphasize their significance.

THE HISTORICAL RELIABILITY OF JOHN

While historical difficulties in the Synoptics generally relate to their similarities, in John the problem is the differences. How can this Gospel portray such a different perspective on the life of the same Jesus? Why are so many episodes unique and so much Synoptic material left out? Why does Jesus speak so differently? Some scholars find these questions so daunting that they construct their portrait of the historical Jesus almost exclusively from the Synoptics. This is to a certain extent understandable, since John is admittedly a more interpretive Gospel than the Synoptics. Yet over the last few decades, there has been an increased respect for the historicity of John.

The Author as Eyewitness. In chapter 10, we noted the compelling evidence that the traditions of the fourth Gospel go back to the eyewitness testimony of the Beloved Disciple and that this individual was most likely the apostle John. The author claims to be an eyewitness (1:14; 19:35; 21:24–25) and provides many eyewitness details one would expect from a Palestinian Jew.

Alleged Contradictions with the Synoptics. Most of the alleged contradictions between John and the Synoptics are quite easily explained by recognizing that John, like the other Gospel writers, abbreviated, arranged, edited, and interpreted his material in such a way as to emphasize particular themes. This editing process means we have different and complementary presentations but not necessarily contradictory ones.

For example, John describes *Mary's* anointing of Jesus' *feet* with perfume *six days* before Passover (John 12:1–8), while Mark describes the anointing of his *head* by an *unnamed woman*, apparently *two days* before Passover (Mark 14:1–9; cf. Matt. 26:6–13). While we could propose two anointings (three counting Luke 7:36–50), the better conclusion is that Mark has rearranged the chronology for theological reasons, to place the episode beside the plot against Jesus in Mark 14:1–2. As the religious leaders wickedly plot Jesus' death, a faithful follower reverently prepares his body for burial. The two days before Passover would then be a reference to the plot against Jesus, not the anointing. The other differences are insignificant. Mark never refers to this Mary (the sister of Martha) elsewhere, and so her name is not important for him here. The anointing of both feet and head would have been a common practice. Mark seems to allow for this when he refers to the anointing of Jesus' *body* for burial (Mark 14:8). As in this case, most apparent contradictions have reasonable explanations when the Evangelists are given appropriate freedom to tell their stories and are unshackled from unreasonable expectations for historical precision.

John's Style and the Words of Jesus. But what about Jesus' unique style of speaking in John? It is certainly true that John is the most interpretive of the Gospels and that the author feels free to explain and elaborate on Jesus' words. Yet it is going beyond the evidence to claim that the discourses are pure fiction. First, we have to remember that the author may use his own style, rather than Jesus' exact words, to provide Jesus' essential message. Second, Jesus tells the disciples that the Spirit will guide them in remembering and understanding his words (John 14:25–26; 15:26–27; 16:14). John's Gospel may at times reflect this Spirit-inspired interpretation.

But third, we must not overstate the differences between Jesus' speech in the Synoptics and in John. A striking statement by Jesus in Matthew 11:27 (cf. Luke 10:22) suggests that Jesus did speak in the manner represented in John: "All things have been committed to me by my Father. No one knows the Son except the Father, and no one knows the Father except the Son and those to whom the Son chooses to reveal him."

These words recall passages like John 3:35; 7:29; 10:14–15; 13:3; 17:2, 25. Similarly, in Mark 9:37, Jesus says, "Whoever welcomes me does not welcome me but *the one who sent me*" (emphasis added; cf. Luke 9:48; 10:16; Matt. 10:40). The language echoes John 12:44 and 13:20, and the phrase "the one who sent me" occurs twenty-three times in John. These passages indicate that John's style may not be imposed on Jesus so much as influenced by the way Jesus actually spoke.

The Christology of John. Finally, we must deal with the exalted Christology of John's Gospel. How do we account for John's explicit affirmations of Jesus' deity (John 1:1; 20:28), when the Synoptics are so much more reserved in this regard? Again, these differences have been overstated. There is little in John that cannot be found implicitly in the Synoptics, where Jesus exercises the attributes of God: forgiving sins (Mark 2:5 par.), reading minds (Mark 2:8 par.; Matt. 12:25), and receiving worship (Matt. 2:11; 14:33; 28:9, 17; Luke 24:52). He is the judge of all humanity, determining people's eternal destiny (Matt. 7:21–23; 25:31–46). Following the resurrection, he mediates the Holy Spirit—the presence of God—to his people (Luke 24:49; Acts 1:5, 8; 2:33) and promises his divine presence among them (Matt. 18:20; 28:20; Acts 16:7).

Nor can it be said that the Synoptic emphasis on Jesus' messiahship is absent in John. As in the Synoptics, Jesus is the Messiah (John 1:41; 4:25–26), the king of Israel (John 1:49; 12:13), and the fulfillment of Old Testament prophecies. As in the Synoptics, he is wholly dependent on the Father and committed to doing his will (John 5:19, 30; 6:38; 8:28; Mark 14:36 par.).

CONCLUSION: THE GOSPELS AS HISTORY AND THEOLOGY

Scholars sometimes assume that if the Gospels were written primarily for theological reasons, they cannot be historically accurate. Yet it is unjustified to assume that theological documents cannot also be historical ones. While the Gospels arose in the context of the needs and concerns of the early church communities and were written to address those needs, the writers also believed that the good news of Jesus Christ was firmly grounded in history. The evidence suggests that the Gospel writers were passionate about preserving the words and deeds of Jesus and that their historical reliability was an essential part of their theological significance. A close examination reveals that good history can also be good theology.

Questions for Review and Discussion

1. Do the faith commitments of the Gospel writers negate their claim to writing accurate history? Why or why not?
2. What is the evidence for a generally reliable Gospel tradition?
3. How might we explain some of the apparent contradictions among the Gospels?

Recommended Resources

Blomberg, Craig. *The Historical Reliability of John's Gospel: Issues and Commentary.* Downers Grove, IL: InterVarsity, 2011.

Blomberg, Craig. *The Historical Reliability of the Gospels.* 2nd ed. Downers Grove, IL: InterVarsity, 2007.

Hemer, C. J. *The Book of Acts in the Setting of Hellenistic History.* Edited by C. H. Gempf. WUNT 2.49. Tübingen: Mohr, 1989.

CHAPTER 13

BEGINNINGS: JESUS' BIRTH AND CHILDHOOD

THE ANCESTRY OF JESUS

The Old Testament predicted that a messianic king would one day arise to reestablish the Davidic dynasty (2 Sam. 7:11–16; Isa. 9:1–7; 11:1–9; Jer. 23:5–6; Ezek. 34:23–24; 37:24–25), and both Matthew and Luke affirm Jesus' Davidic ancestry. In addition to identifying Jesus' father, Joseph, as a descendant of David (Matt. 1:20; Luke 1:27; 2:4), both provide genealogies linking Jesus to David's line (Matt. 1:1–17; Luke 3:23–38). The genealogies have a number of important differences. Matthew's proceeds temporally from Abraham to Jesus, while Luke's moves backward from Jesus all the way to Adam. This descent to Adam is likely related to Luke's desire to identify Jesus with salvation for all humanity. While the genealogies are essentially the same from Abraham to David, from David to Jesus they are different. Luke's list is much longer, containing forty names between David and Joseph, compared with Matthew's twenty-six. This can be explained by the common practice of abbreviating genealogies. As noted in chapter 4, Matthew seems to skip generations in order to structure his genealogy around groups of fourteen generations. More problematic are the different names. Matthew follows the line of David's son Solomon, while Luke follows the line of Nathan, another son of David. This discrepancy has been explained in a variety of ways:

1. Some consider one or both genealogies to be unhistorical, created by Christians to provide Jesus with a Davidic lineage and legitimate messianic credentials. While this is possible, independent

attestation of Jesus' Davidic ancestry is provided by Mark (Mark 10:47–48), Paul (Rom. 1:3; 2 Tim. 2:8), the author of Hebrews (Heb. 7:14), and John (Rev. 5:5; 22:16).

2. The traditional solution to the two genealogies is that Luke provides Mary's, while Matthew gives Joseph's. Evidence for this is Luke's emphasis on Mary throughout his birth narrative. One problem with this view is that Luke's list begins with Joseph, who seems to be identified as the son of Heli. Another is that throughout Luke's birth narrative, it is Joseph's, not Mary's, Davidic descent which is stressed (Luke 1:27; 2:4).

3. Another common solution is that both genealogies are related to Joseph, but while Matthew presents a royal or legal genealogy (the official line of Davidic kings), Luke lists Joseph's actual physical ancestors.

4. A whole range of ingenious proposals explain how Joseph could have two genealogies. Some say Mary had no brothers to carry on her father Heli's name, so at her marriage, Heli adopted Joseph as his own son and heir. More complex solutions appeal to the Old Testament laws of *levirate marriage*, whereby the brother of a man who died childless would marry his widow to produce heirs for him (Deut. 25:5–10). In this case, Heli and Jacob were either brothers or half brothers. When one died, the other married his widow, producing Joseph as his offspring. This would leave Joseph with two fathers, a natural one and a legal one, and therefore two genealogies.

With so many possibilities, it is impossible to be dogmatic about any one solution or to confidently reject or confirm its historicity. What can be affirmed is that there was widespread recognition of Jesus' Davidic ancestry within the early church.

THE VIRGINAL CONCEPTION

Both Matthew and Luke claim that Mary became pregnant during the period of her engagement to Joseph and that this was accomplished through the Holy Spirit (Matt. 1:18–25; Luke 1:26–38). Traditionally called the "virgin birth," the event is better termed a *virginal conception*, since the conception was miraculous and the birth was apparently normal. The historicity of the virginal conception was a major issue of scholarly debate in the nineteenth and twentieth centuries. Skeptics claimed that the story arose through syncretism with pagan stories related to gods impregnating human women or that it was created by later Christians to provide a "fulfillment" of Isaiah 7:14.

Yet the biblical account is very different from pagan myths, with no hint of a sexual union between Mary and the Holy Spirit. Most scholars have abandoned such appeals to pagan parallels. That the virginal conception is not a late addition to the Gospel story is suggested by its independent attestation in Matthew and Luke and by possible allusions to it elsewhere in the New Testament (Mark 6:3; John 8:4; Gal. 4:4).

What is the theological significance of the virginal conception? Some have argued it was necessary to protect Jesus' sinless nature, but the narratives themselves do not indicate this purpose. The Messiah could have entered human life free from sin with or without a virginal conception. Nor is Scripture explicit on the details of the conception. Did God create the sperm for Mary's egg? Did he create a fertilized embryo? In the final analysis, the details remain a mystery. What is certain from the text is that the conception of Jesus was a supernatural act of God, confirming that God himself was about to accomplish the salvation that no human being could achieve.

BETHLEHEM BIRTHPLACE

Though Jesus was raised in Nazareth, Matthew and Luke identify Jesus' birthplace as Bethlehem (Matt. 2:1; Luke 2:4–7). Bethlehem's theological significance is as the birthplace and hometown of David, Israel's greatest king and the prototype of the Messiah (1 Samuel 16; 2 Samuel 7). Micah 5:2–5 predicts that a great ruler will come from Bethlehem, a new David who will shepherd God's people and bring peace and security to the nation. Matthew links Jesus' Bethlehem birth to the fulfillment of this prophecy (Matt. 2:6), while Luke connects it more generally with Jesus' Davidic lineage and his role as the Messiah (Luke 2:4, 11).

Critics often deny that Bethlehem was Jesus' birthplace, claiming that the title Jesus of Nazareth is evidence that Jesus was really from Nazareth in Galilee and that the Bethlehem story was created to "fulfill" Micah 5:2. However, both Matthew and Luke attest to the birthplace independently. (See also the ironic reference in John 7:42.) Luke does not even link Bethlehem to the Micah passage, suggesting that it was a part of the tradition distinct from this fulfillment motif.

THE CENSUS

According to Luke, the event that brought Jesus' family to Bethlehem was a census conducted by the emperor Caesar Augustus (Luke 2:1). While censuses for tax purposes were common in the Roman Empire, there are several historical problems with this one.

First, we have no other evidence of a single empire-wide census under Augustus. Would not such a major event have left a record in Roman history? In fact, this is not a major difficulty. We know that Augustus reorganized the administration of the empire and conducted numerous local censuses. Luke is probably treating a local Palestinian census as part of Augustus's empire-wide reorganization of the provinces.

A second problem is that Luke says this was the first census while Quirinius was governor of Syria (2:2). According to Josephus, Quirinius's governorship began in AD 6, ten years too late for Jesus' birth. Various solutions are possible here. There is some evidence that Quirinius may have held a prior governorship or at least a broad administrative position over Syria at the time of Jesus' birth. Others have suggested that Luke is referring to a census completed by Quirinius but begun by an earlier governor. Still others note that the Greek word for "first" *(prōtē)* may be translated "before," so that Luke is saying this census took place *before* Quirinius's governorship of Syria.

In short, while there are some problems related to the census, there is not enough evidence to either refute or confirm Luke's claim. Considering his historical accuracy elsewhere, his statement should be given the benefit of the doubt.

THE BIRTH OF JESUS

A careful reading of the birth narrative produces a picture quite different from the traditional Christmas pageant, in which shepherds, wise men, angels, and farm animals all crowd into a stable around the holy family. The text does not say that Jesus was born on the night Mary and Joseph arrived in Bethlehem; rather it indicates he was born sometime during their stay there (Luke 2:6). The "inn" *(katalyma)* was probably not an ancient hotel with an innkeeper, since a small village like Bethlehem would not have had such accommodations. Luke uses a different Greek word in Luke 10:34 for a roadside inn *(pandocheion)*. The word *katalyma* normally means either a guest room in a private residence or a caravansary, an informal public shelter where travelers would gather for the night. The most likely scenario is that Joseph and Mary were staying with relatives or friends and, because of crowded conditions, were forced to a place reserved for animals. This could have been a lower-level stall attached to the living quarters of the home or, as some ancient traditions suggest, a cave used as a shelter for animals. The "manger" where Jesus was laid was a feeding trough for animals, and the traditional "swaddling clothes" were strips of cloth intended to keep the limbs straight, a sign of motherly care and affection (Ezek. 16:4).

While Luke recounts the angelic announcement to humble shepherds in the hills around Bethlehem, Matthew tells of magi, or wise men, who came from the east. Contrary to the traditional manger scene, Matthew does not say there were three magi (the number three comes from the three gifts) or that they arrived with the shepherds on the night of Jesus' birth. Mary and Joseph are living in a house in Bethlehem when they come (2:11), and Herod the Great tries to kill all the male children in Bethlehem two years of age and under (2:16), indicating that Jesus may have been as old as two. The magi were probably Persian or Arabian astrologers (not kings, as is sometimes supposed) who charted the stars and attached religious significance to their movements.

Warned in a dream of Herod's evil intention to kill the child, Joseph escapes with the family to Egypt, where they remain until the death of Herod. While the historian Josephus does not mention Herod's massacre of the infants of Bethlehem, this is not surprising since Bethlehem was a small village and the number of children could not have been large. Considering Herod's many ruthless actions in murdering sons, wives, and all manner of political opponents, this event was of little historical consequence to first-century historians.

When Joseph is informed in a dream that Herod has died, he returns with Mary and Jesus to Israel. Hearing that Herod's cruel and incompetent son Archelaus is ruling in Judea, he moves the family to Nazareth in Galilee, where Jesus grows up.

JESUS' FAMILY LIFE

According to the Gospels, Jesus had four brothers—James, Joseph, Judas, and Simon—and at least two sisters (Mark 6:3; Matt. 13:55–56). There is a lively debate concerning the actual relationship of these siblings. Roman Catholic theologians have traditionally claimed that these are not true brothers and sisters but cousins. This is usually suggested to protect the perpetual virginity of Mary. But Greek has a distinct word for cousin (*anepsios*, Col. 4:10), making this view unlikely.

A second view is that these are children from a previous marriage of Joseph, who was a widower. This is possible, and there are some indications that Joseph may have been somewhat older than Mary. He never appears during Jesus' public ministry, and so likely died before Jesus began to preach. But if these are children from a previous marriage, it is odd that no mention is made of them in the birth narrative. The most likely explanation is that these are the siblings of Jesus born to Mary and Joseph after the birth of Jesus.

The Gospels portray Mary and Joseph as faithful and pious Jews (Matt. 1:19; Luke 1:28–30, 38; 2:21–24). Jesus' father was a carpenter (Matt. 13:55), and like most children of his day, Jesus followed in his father's career (Mark 6:3). The Greek term translated "carpenter" *(tektōn)* is a general one, referring to someone who built with materials like stone, wood, or metal. Joseph and his sons may have been primarily stonemasons, building homes and public buildings. The family's social status would have been low, since they were among the working poor, though there is no evidence that they were destitute.

Nazareth, while only a small village, was located just a few miles from the major Hellenistic-Jewish city of Sepphoris. It is possible that Joseph and his sons found work in this commercial center. This would have given Jesus some exposure to Greek-speaking people and Greco-Roman city life. Like most Jewish boys, Jesus would have been educated in the local synagogue, where he learned the Scriptures and the Hebrew language. We know from his Nazareth sermon that he could read Hebrew (Luke 4:16–20). This means Jesus was probably trilingual, speaking Aramaic in the home and with friends, using Hebrew in religious contexts, and conversing in Greek in business and governmental contexts.

Apart from these generalities, we know almost nothing about Jesus' early life. To be sure, later Christians composed *infancy gospels*, fanciful accounts of Jesus' boyhood that turned him into a child prodigy and miracle worker. For example, the late second-century *Infancy Gospel of Thomas* has the boy Jesus making clay pigeons fly and lengthening beams in Joseph's carpentry shop. Such stories have no historical foundation. Jesus no doubt had a rather ordinary childhood as a Jewish boy growing up in a conservative Israelite household.

The only biblical account from Jesus' childhood comes from Luke, who describes his growth toward physical and spiritual maturity and illustrates this with a Passover visit to Jerusalem when Jesus was twelve years old (Luke 2:40–52). Jewish tradition held that a boy became responsible to observe the law when he was thirteen years old (though the bar mitzvah ceremony is of later origin). By taking Jesus to Jerusalem to celebrate Passover, his parents are preparing him for his covenant responsibilities. The family would have traveled from Nazareth to Jerusalem—a journey of four or five days—in a caravan of relatives and friends for protection. This explains how Jesus' parents could have left him behind in Jerusalem, assuming he was with friends. When his anxious parents finally discover him in the temple, he is sitting at the feet of the Jewish teachers, who marvel at his wisdom. His question, "Didn't you know I had to be in my Father's house?" confirms a growing awareness of his special father-son relationship with God. Though conclusions about Jesus' childhood self-consciousness are speculative, Luke claims that by puberty he had a growing awareness of the special role he would play in God's plan.

Questions for Review and Discussion

1. What are the main differences between the genealogies of Matthew and Luke? How might we explain these differences?

2. What is the theological significance of Jesus' birth in Bethlehem?
3. What do we know about Jesus' family?

Recommended Resources

Brown, Raymond E. *The Birth of the Messiah: A Commentary on the Infancy Narratives in the Gospels of Matthew and Luke.* Updated ed. New Haven, CT: Yale Univ. Press, 1999.

Laurentin, René. *The Truth of Christmas beyond the Myths: The Gospels of the Infancy of Christ.* Translated by Michael J. Wrenn et al. Petersham, MA: St. Bede's, 1986.

Machen, J. Gresham. *The Virgin Birth of Christ.* New York: Harper, 1930.

CHAPTER 14

PREPARING FOR MINISTRY

JOHN THE BAPTIST, HERALD OF MESSIANIC SALVATION

All four Gospels link the beginning of Jesus' ministry with the appearance of John the Baptist (Matt. 3:1–12; Mark 1:1–8; Luke 3:1–20; John 1:6–8, 15, 19–36). John's role is explained with prophecies from Isaiah 40 and Malachi 3 and 4. He is the "voice of one calling: 'In the wilderness prepare the way for the Lord'" (Isa. 40:3) and the Elijah-like messenger who will prepare God's people for the day of the Lord (Mal. 3:1; 4:5–6; Matt. 11:14; 17:12).

Only Luke's Gospel provides information concerning John's early life. He was born to Zechariah and Elizabeth, pious Jews of priestly descent (Luke 1:5–6, 39–40). Zechariah served as priest in the Jerusalem temple, and Elizabeth was a relative of Jesus' mother, Mary (1:36). Elizabeth was old and childless until God miraculously intervened and she became pregnant. John's special prophetic role was presaged when Mary visited Elizabeth and the baby "leaped for joy" in Elizabeth's womb (1:41–44). What, if any, contact John and Jesus had before their public ministries is unknown, since Jesus was raised in Galilee and John in Judea.

After the account of John's birth, Luke mentions only that John "grew and became strong in spirit; and he lived in the wilderness until he appeared publicly to Israel" (1:80). Some have speculated from this desert lifestyle that John may have had contact with the monastic community at Qumran near the Dead Sea. In an intriguing comment, Josephus writes that the Essenes "neglect wedlock, but choose out other persons' children, while they are pliable, and fit for learning, and esteem them to be of their kindred, and form them according to their own manners" (*J.W.* 2.8.2 §§120–21). If John's elderly parents died before he reached adulthood, it is possible that he was raised by this community. John's message has interesting points in common with the beliefs of the Qumran sect. Both John and the Essenes shared a strong expectation of the imminent arrival of God's final salvation; both used the prophecy of Isaiah 40:3 (1QS 8:14); both identified themselves with the righteous remnant called out from apostate Israel; and both practiced ritual washings of some sort. Unfortunately, there is not nearly enough evidence to confirm this fascinating hypothesis.

Since he was born shortly before Jesus (Luke 1), John was probably about thirty when his ministry began. He is portrayed as carrying on an itinerant preaching ministry in the Judean wilderness and baptizing people in the Jordan River.

John must have been a striking figure, emerging from the wilderness dressed in camel skin and a leather belt (Mark 1:6), garb reminiscent of the prophet Elijah (2 Kings 1:8). His diet of locusts and wild honey, though strange today, was typical of ascetics who lived off the land. The Dead Sea Scrolls even provide instructions on how to eat locusts (CD 12:13).

John preached a "baptism of repentance for the forgiveness of sins," warning people to repent in light of the coming fiery judgment of God (Mark 1:4, 7–8; Luke 3:3, 15–18). Josephus describes John's baptism as a symbolic purification of the body which followed the purification of the soul by righteousness (*Ant.* 18.5.2 §117). The background to this baptism has been a matter of much debate. Some have seen parallels to the ceremonial washings practiced by the Essenes and other Jewish groups. As an act of ceremonial cleansing, individuals would dip themselves into a *mikveh*, or immersion pool. At Qumran, such washings, like John's, represented a turning from sin to participate in the end-time community of God (1QS 5:13–14). Yet John's baptism is different in that it appears to be a onetime event rather than a repeated ritual. Others have pointed to the Jewish practice of proselyte (new convert) baptism, in which case John may be calling the apostate nation to become true Israel once again. While this fits the message of John, it is unclear whether proselyte baptism was practiced by Jews in the first century. John's baptism is perhaps best viewed as his unique eschatological application of cleansing and initiatory rituals found in first-century Judaism.

According to the Gospels, John explicitly denied messianic claims and announced that one "more powerful" was coming after him (Mark 1:7–8; Matt. 3:11–12; Luke 3:15–18; John 1:24–28; 3:23–36). While John baptized with water, this messianic figure would baptize with the Holy Spirit and with fire. Some argue that this baptism refers to two distinct events, a Spirit baptism for the righteous and a fire baptism for the wicked. More likely, John refers to one Spirit-and-fire baptism that purifies the righteous and judges the wicked. Isaiah 4:4 speaks in an eschatological context of a "spirit of judgment and a spirit of fire" that will "cleanse the bloodstains from Jerusalem" (cf. Mal. 3:2).

Some scholars have claimed that historically John's ministry had nothing to do with Jesus but that John was expecting God himself to come and bring in the day of the Lord. It was later Christians who transformed John into the forerunner of the Messiah. Yet the evidence suggests otherwise. John's statement about being unworthy to untie the sandals of the Messiah (attested independently in the Synoptics and the fourth Gospel, Mark 1:7 par.; John 1:27) suggests that John was expecting a human successor. Similarly, John's later doubts about Jesus are inexplicable unless he already had some messianic expectations concerning him (Luke 7:18–35; Matt. 11:2–19). It is unlikely that the church would create an episode in which John raised doubts about Jesus' messianic status.

Jesus identifies John as the last and greatest of the Old Testament prophets, indeed the greatest person ever born. Yet, paradoxically, "the one who is least in the kingdom of God is greater than he" (Luke 7:28; Matt. 11:11; cf. Luke 16:16). The meaning of this paradox may be that while John announced the age of salvation, he did not see its establishment. The "least in the kingdom" are those who are blessed to live in the age of fulfillment, with the new life imparted through Jesus' resurrection and the indwelling presence of the Holy Spirit. While John was the herald of the new age of salvation, Jesus was its inaugurator.

John's challenge to the status quo eventually led to his death. According to Mark, Herod Antipas imprisoned John when he spoke out against Herod's divorce and subsequent marriage to Herodias, his brother Philip's wife. Such a marriage was viewed as incestuous by pious Jews (Lev. 18:16; 20:21). While Herod was fascinated by John and reluctant to execute him, he was provoked into doing so by his wife Herodias (Mark 6:17–29; cf. Matt. 14:1–12). Josephus also refers to John's arrest and execution but attributes it more generally to Herod's fear that John would provoke an uprising (*Ant.* 18.5.2 §§116–19). There is no contradiction here, since Josephus gives the political reason for the arrest, while Mark provides the specific circumstances of the execution.

The movement begun by John continued after his death, and followers of the Baptist appear later in the book of Acts (Acts 18:25; 19:1–7).

THE BAPTISM OF JESUS

The baptism of Jesus marks the beginning of his public ministry. Apart from the crucifixion, it is perhaps the least disputed historical event of Jesus' life. Even radical skeptics accept that Jesus was baptized by John, since the church would hardly have invented a story in which Jesus appears to submit to the authority of John. Jesus' baptism and the descent of the Spirit are narrated in the three Synoptics (Matt. 3:13–17; Mark 1:9–11; Luke 3:21–22) and alluded to in John (John 1:29–34).

Why did Jesus submit to John's baptism of repentance? Only Matthew suggests a reason. When John resists Jesus' request for baptism, Jesus responds that it should be done "to fulfill all righteousness" (Matt. 3:15). Righteousness here probably means faithful submission to God's purpose. In this way, Jesus connects his ministry with John's and associates himself with those who are responding in repentance to John's preaching.

The Spirit's descent and the voice from heaven have sometimes been described as a vision experienced by Jesus alone, although John 1:32 indicates that John the Baptist also witnessed them. If Jesus' willingness to be baptized represented his identification with repentant Israel, the descent of the Spirit provided the empowerment to accomplish his messianic task. Luke in particular identifies the Spirit's descent as Jesus' anointing as Messiah (Luke 3:21–22; 4:1, 14, 18).

The descent of the Spirit "as a dove" (John 1:32) may mean that the Spirit looked like a dove or merely that the descent was similar to a bird's flight. The symbolism has been widely discussed. Some see an allusion to Genesis 1:2, where the Spirit hovers over the waters at creation. Jesus could here be identified with the new creation. Others suggest an allusion to Genesis 8:8–12, where Noah's dove represents God's gracious deliverance after judgment.

The voice from heaven signifies the Father's affirmation of Jesus' person and mission. "You are my Son" alludes to Psalm 2:7, where God announces the Messiah's divine sonship and legitimate rule from Mount Zion. "With you I am well pleased" echoes Isaiah 42:1, where the faithful and suffering Servant of the LORD is identified as God's chosen one. Finally, "whom I love" may represent an Isaac-Jesus typology from Genesis 22:2, where Isaac is Abraham's only son "whom you love." Abraham's willingness to offer his beloved son would be analogous to God's offering of his Son. If all three allusions are present, this single announcement makes the extraordinary claim that Jesus is the promised Messiah who will offer himself as a sacrifice for his people.

THE TEMPTATION OF JESUS

All three Synoptics connect Jesus' baptism with the temptation of Jesus in the wilderness. Empowered by the Spirit as Messiah at his baptism, Jesus is led into the wilderness to be tempted by Satan (Matt. 4:1–11; Mark 1:12–13; Luke 4:1–13). The main theme of the temptation is the obedience of the Son to the will of the Father. Will Jesus submit to the purpose of the Father, or will he pursue the path of personal glory? Satan repeatedly tempts Jesus to exploit his position as the Son of God for his own gain.

While Mark merely states that the temptation took place, Matthew and Luke detail three incidents. These three are analogous to the experience of Israel in the wilderness. While God's "son" Israel (Ex. 4:22–23) failed when tested in the wilderness, Jesus the true Son remains obedient and emerges victorious. Jesus' forty days are analogous to Israel's forty years, and the three Old Testament passages Jesus cites all relate to Israel's failures in the desert. Israel was tested with hunger so that they would learn dependence on God, but they constantly complained. Jesus depends wholly on God for his sustenance, quoting Deuteronomy 8:3: "Man does not live on bread alone" (Matt. 4:4; Luke 4:4). Israel doubted God's power and put him to the test at Massah. Jesus refuses to throw himself from the temple and so test the Lord God, citing Deuteronomy 6:16: "Do not put the Lord your God to the test" (Matt. 4:7; Luke 4:12). Finally, Israel was commanded to worship God alone but turned to idolatry (Deut. 9:12; Judg. 3:5–7). Jesus rejects the devil's offer of the kingdoms of the world in exchange for his worship, quoting Deuteronomy 6:13: "Worship the Lord your God, and serve him only" (Matt. 4:10; Luke 4:8). As the Messiah and Son of God, Jesus represents the nation of Israel and succeeds where they failed. He will now fulfill Israel's Old Testament mandate, revealing God's glory and taking the message of salvation to the ends of the earth.

An Adam-Jesus typology may also be present in the temptation account, with Jesus resisting the temptation to which Adam and Eve succumbed. The presence of Satan as the personal tempter would be analogous to the serpent's temptation of Eve. In this case, Jesus is the second Adam who will reverse the results of the fall. Mark's reference to the wild beasts (Mark 1:13) may play on this Eden theme. Luke's genealogy, which appears just before his temptation account, identifies Adam as the "son of God" (Luke 3:38). Where Adam the first son of God was tested and failed, Jesus the true Son of God succeeds.

The historicity of the temptation has been doubted by some, but there are good reasons for accepting that the story originated with Jesus himself. There are no clear parallels to such an encounter with Satan in the Old Testament or Judaism, and no good reason why the early church would create such an account. The kind of messianic temptations Jesus experienced were unique to his mission, not the common experience of believers.

Concerning its nature, the temptation may have been at least partly visionary, an experience which Jesus later recounted to his disciples. Luke suggests a visionary dimension when he says that Satan showed Jesus all the kingdoms of the world "in an instant" (Luke 4:5). Whether the temptations were visionary or not, the Gospels present them as real temptations from a personal Satan, part of Jesus' preparation for his messianic ministry.

Questions for Review and Discussion

1. What role does John the Baptist play in the Gospel tradition?
2. What is the significance of the Old Testament allusions in the voice from heaven at Jesus' baptism?
3. What is the main theme of the temptation account?

Recommended Resources

Beasley-Murray, G. R. *Baptism in the New Testament.* Grand Rapids: Eerdmans, 1962.

Gibson, Jeffrey B. *The Temptations of Jesus in Early Christianity.* Sheffield: Sheffield Academic Press, 1995.

Webb, Robert. *John the Baptizer and Prophet: A Socio-historical Study.* Sheffield: JSOT Press, 1991.

CHAPTER 15

JESUS' MESSAGE

JESUS THE TEACHER

The Gospels confirm that Jesus was a teacher with extraordinary gifts. Mark notes that "the people were amazed at his teaching, because he taught them as one who had authority, not as the teachers of the law" (Mark 1:22). The scribes of Jesus' day taught with constant appeal to the traditions of the past, referring to legal precedents set by the rabbis before them. In contrast, Jesus taught with a sense of originality and personal authority.

Jesus' teaching style also captivated his audience. He spoke in down-to-earth language with stories drawn from everyday life. He used a range of literary devices, including proverbs, metaphors, similes, riddles, puns, hyperbole, paradox, and irony. Who can forget Jesus' striking hyperbole of a camel trying to squeeze its enormous snout through the tiny eye of a needle (Mark 10:25 par.) or the bizarre scene of a person trying to take a tiny splinter from a friend's eye while ignoring the enormous beam sticking out of their own (Matt. 7:3–5)? Such imagery caught the imagination of the people, causing them to hang on to his every word.

JESUS' CENTRAL MESSAGE: THE KINGDOM OF GOD

When Jesus began preaching in Galilee, his message concerned the coming of the kingdom of God (Mark 1:15; cf. Matt. 4:17; Luke 4:43).

The Jewish Background. Two ideas about God's kingdom existed side by side in Judaism. The first was God's ever-present reign as king over all the earth. God's kingdom has no boundaries. It is universal and eternal: "Your kingdom is an everlasting kingdom, and your dominion endures through all generations" (Ps. 145:13).

Though God is now king, other passages speak of a day when he will establish his kingdom on earth. Isaiah 24:23 describes a time when "the LORD Almighty will reign on Mount Zion and in Jerusalem, and before its elders—with great glory" (cf. Zech. 14:9). Both ideas—the universal and the future reigns of God—appear in the Old Testament and in the Jewish literature of Jesus' day. In much of the apocalyptic literature, the persecuted people of God long for the day when he will intervene to defeat their enemies and establish his reign on earth. The present evil age will then pass into the age to come, a time of glory, justice, and righteousness for Israel.

Jesus and the Kingdom. Jesus' preaching acknowledged both senses of the kingdom of God. In the present, God is the sovereign Lord of the universe, who feeds the birds of the air and clothes the lilies of the field (Matt. 6:26–30). People are to "seek first his kingdom" by submitting to his sovereign authority (Matt. 6:33).

Yet Jesus also taught that the kingdom of God was a future state that believers would one day enter (Mark 9:47; Matt. 7:21; 25:34). He referred to a time when his disciples would know that the kingdom was near (Luke 21:31). The coming of the kingdom would mean the judgment of the wicked (Matt. 25:41), the establishment of a redeemed community founded on righteousness and justice (Matt. 13:36–43), and perfect fellowship with God (Luke 13:28–29; Matt. 8:11). God's instrument in the establishment of this future kingdom is the Son of Man, who will return and gather God's chosen people from the ends of the earth (Mark 13:26–27 par.; cf. Luke 17:20–37; Matt. 16:27–28). In these contexts, the kingdom of God is synonymous with the age to come, when God will judge the wicked and vindicate his people.

What was radically unique about Jesus' teaching was his claim that this end-times kingdom of God was even now arriving through his own words and actions. Jesus announces that the kingdom of God has "come near" (Mark 1:14–15). While Judaism saw the eschatological kingdom coming at the end of the age, Jesus proclaimed that God was acting now to reveal his kingdom and defeat Satan. When accused by the Pharisees of casting out demons by Satan's power, Jesus points to the real source of his authority: "If I drive out demons by the finger of God, *then the kingdom of God has come upon you*" (Luke

11:20, emphasis added; cf. Matt. 12:28). Jesus' exorcisms reveal the kingdom by asserting God's reign over the authority of Satan.

We must therefore acknowledge both present and future dimensions in Jesus' kingdom preaching. The kingdom is both already and not yet. In the present, people are called to submit to God's authority and so "enter" his kingdom (Mark 10:15, 23–25; Matt. 21:31; 23:13; Luke 11:52; 18:16–17). When they do, they freely receive God's salvation benefits available through Jesus Christ (Matt. 25:34). Yet while Jesus inaugurated the kingdom at his first coming, he will consummate it at his return (Mark 13:26–27 par.). Satan was defeated in the ministry of Jesus and at the cross, but his final destruction awaits the end.

JESUS AND THE LAW: THE ETHICS OF THE KINGDOM

Jesus called people not only to acknowledge God's kingdom but also to submit to it in their daily lives. The inauguration of the kingdom creates a new way of life and a radical new kingdom ethic. How does this new ethic relate to the law of Moses that governed Israel's national life? We examined this question in chapter 5 from the perspective of Matthew's theology. Here we will expand on that discussion with reference to Jesus' kingdom program.

On the one hand, Jesus affirmed the eternal validity of the law, stating that not the smallest letter would disappear from it until everything was fulfilled (Matt. 5:18–20). On the other hand, Jesus seemed to ignore and even alter aspects of the law. In Mark 7:18–19, Jesus apparently cancels the dietary laws of the Old Testament. How do we harmonize these seemingly contradictory statements? Did Jesus abolish the law or affirm it? In response, two points should be kept in mind: (1) Jesus' emphasis on the true essence of the law, and (2) his role as the fulfillment of the law.

The True Essence of the Law. Much of Jesus' teaching challenges the legalistic and sometimes hypocritical manner in which the law was applied. He criticizes the Pharisees and scribes for tithing the smallest of spices yet neglecting the fundamental aspects of the law, like justice, mercy, and faithfulness (Matt. 23:23; Luke 11:42). When challenged because his disciples did not practice Jewish ceremonial washings,

Jesus quoted Isaiah 29:13: "These people honor me with their lips, but their hearts are far from me. . . . Their teachings are merely human rules" (Mark 7:6–7; cf. Matt. 15:1–9). Jesus is not here condemning the Pharisees simply because they have traditions. The purpose of their oral law was a noble one: to apply God's commandments to the new and changing circumstances of everyday life. Jesus condemns them rather for ignoring the true spirit and purpose of the law.

This is seen in Jesus' apparent disregard for Sabbath traditions. When challenged by the Pharisees, Jesus reminds them that "the Sabbath was made for man, not man for the Sabbath" (Mark 2:27). The scribes and Pharisees had turned the Sabbath into a burden to bear rather than a gift from God to enjoy.

The true essence of the law is also the key to the six antitheses of the Sermon on the Mount (Matt. 5:21–48), in which Jesus pushes beyond the external requirements to the true intention of God. It is not just murder that is a sin (Ex. 20:13) but anger, which is murder of the heart (Matt. 5:21–26). The command against adultery (Ex. 20:14) extends to lust, adultery of the heart (Matt. 5:27–30). Love should be shown not only to your neighbor (Lev. 19:18) but even to your enemies. This reflects the heart of God, who shows kindness even to sinners (Matt. 5:43–48). This radical new ethic is ultimately neither radical nor new but wholly in line with the character of God, whose kingdom Jesus is announcing.

Jesus as Fulfillment of the Law. While much of Jesus' teaching brings out the true meaning of the law, other teaching suggests a radical new orientation to the law. How do we account for the early church's freedom from compulsion to worship on the Sabbath (Saturday) or to observe the Old Testament dietary laws? The answer must be found in Jesus' role not just as the interpreter of the law but also as its fulfillment.

To understand this, we must look to the Old Testament background. Although Israel repeatedly broke God's law, God promised to one day establish a *new covenant* that would provide forgiveness of sins, knowledge of God, and the law written on their hearts (Jer. 31:31–34). This new covenant cannot be separated from Jesus' announcement of the kingdom. At the Last Supper, Jesus explicitly links his death to the establishment of the new covenant and the coming of the kingdom (Mark 14:24–25; Matt. 26:28–29; Luke 22:20; 1 Cor. 11:25).

How did Jesus fulfill the law? To answer this, we must understand the twofold purpose of the law: (1) to reveal God's righteous standards, and (2) to provide the means of forgiveness when Israel failed to meet those standards. God's people were to be holy because God was holy. When they failed, forgiveness was possible through repentance and the sacrificial system established in the law.

Jesus fulfilled the first purpose of the law in two ways: (1) in his teaching, he interpreted the true meaning of the law, and (2) in his conduct, he lived a life of perfect righteousness. He fulfilled the second purpose by becoming "a ransom for many" through his sacrificial death—the blood of the covenant (Mark 10:45; 14:22–24). Through his sacrificial death, Jesus received the condemnation of the law and paid the penalty for humanity's sins (Rom. 3:25; 8:3–4; 2 Cor. 5:21; Heb. 10:10; 1 Peter 3:18; 1 John 2:2).

What, then, did Jesus mean when he said that no part of the law would disappear until all was accomplished (Matt. 5:17–18)? The answer is that the law is not abolished, but its purpose and function are transformed ("fulfilled") with the coming of Jesus and the kingdom of God. The law continues to reveal God's righteous character and to play a prophetic role in pointing to Christ (Luke 24:25–27, 45–47). But the individual regulations of the law are not binding on believers, because they no longer live under the Mosaic covenant but now live under the new covenant. God's righteous standards are now written on their hearts, not on tablets of stone. Their relationship with God is mediated not through the written law but through the one who fulfilled the law, Jesus the Messiah, and through the Spirit he has given.

GRACE AND WORKS: THE FREE GIFT AND THE COST OF DISCIPLESHIP

The age of the Spirit is the age of grace, and God's free gift of salvation to sinners is a leading theme in Jesus' teaching. Jesus dines with sinners, a symbol of God's gracious acceptance. People enter the kingdom not through works of righteousness but through repentance and faith. Jesus calls for faith like a child's—humble dependence on God (Mark 10:14–15 par.; Matt. 11:25 par.; 18:3). The sinful woman who anoints Jesus' feet is forgiven much, and so loves much (Luke 7:36–50). The prodigal son is received back by the loving father without working off his debt (Luke 15:11–32). The tax collector in the temple is forgiven through humble repentance (Luke 18:9–14). The repentant criminal on the cross is offered a place in paradise despite having no opportunity for good works (Luke 23:39–43). The gospel of Jesus is a gospel of grace offered to sinners.

Yet beside these statements of God's free forgiveness are those about the high cost of discipleship. Jesus calls for his disciples to leave everything and follow him. They are to deny themselves, take up their cross, and follow him (Mark 8:34–38 par.; Luke 14:27; Matt. 10:38). How do we reconcile statements of salvation as a free gift and statements of the high cost of discipleship? The answer must lie in the difference between entrance into the kingdom—a free gift offered to sinners—and the standards expected of those whose lives have been transformed by the Spirit's power. The radical self-sacrificial lifestyle to which Jesus calls his disciples is the consequence of, not the condition for, a life transformed by the Spirit of God.

SOCIAL JUSTICE: THE RICH AND THE POOR

Hand in hand with God's attribute of love are attributes of mercy and justice. Like the words of the Old Testament prophets, Jesus' teaching is full of admonitions for a just and merciful society. He preaches good news to the poor and reaches out to society's outcasts—sinners, lepers, Samaritans, Gentiles, women, and children. He strongly warns of the destructive power of riches. The Beatitudes in Luke pronounce not only blessings on the poor and oppressed but woes against the rich and self-sufficient (Luke 6:20–26; cf. Matt. 5:3–12). Many parables and stories speak of the reversal of fortunes that the kingdom brings (see Luke 12:15–21; 16:19–31).

Is Jesus speaking in these contexts of physical poverty, or is this language metaphorical, referring to those who are spiritually poor? While there are certainly spiritual dimensions in Jesus' teaching on poverty, it is impossible to exclude the physical from Jesus' concrete illustrations. Those who are physically poor and oppressed are naturally driven to greater trust in and dependence on God. Conversely, those who treat riches as their own, rather than as entrusted resources for God's service, live in defiance of his sovereignty. It *is* impossible for a rich man to enter the kingdom of God, since by definition a rich man is one who views his riches as his own. Yet while it is impossible for people, Jesus adds, "All things are possible with God" (Mark 10:17–27 par.). Salvation comes through renunciation of all human effort and achievement—including wealth—and through humble dependence on God.

Questions for Review and Discussion

1. What did Jesus mean by the "kingdom of God," and how do the present and future dimensions of the kingdom relate to one another?
2. Did Jesus affirm the validity of the Old Testament law, or did he overrule the law? What is the solution to this apparent paradox?
3. How can we reconcile Jesus' teaching on God's free grace offered to sinners and his teaching on the high cost of discipleship?

Recommended Resources

Beasley-Murray, G. R. *Jesus and the Kingdom of God.* Grand Rapids: Eerdmans, 1986.

Ladd, G. E. *The Presence of the Future.* Grand Rapids: Eerdmans, 1996.

Stein, Robert H. *The Method and Message of Jesus' Teachings.* Louisville: Westminster John Knox, 1994.

CHAPTER 16

JESUS' MIRACLES

THE QUESTION OF MIRACLES

Many of the negative conclusions concerning the historical Jesus can be traced to a naturalistic worldview. The scientific method that developed during the Enlightenment in the seventeenth and eighteenth centuries sought cause-and-effect relationships for all that occurred in the natural world. Alongside this method arose the philosophies of deism and materialism. Deists claimed that God created the ordered world and then left it to run by natural laws—as a clock is wound up by its maker. Philosophical materialism asserts that the world is a closed system of cause and effect without outside intervention. In this mechanistic worldview, miracles are treated as contrary to the laws of nature and so impossible.

The problem with this claim is that it assumes its own conclusion and confuses the scientific method with philosophical materialism. As a philosophy, materialism asserts that all of reality can be explained through the natural laws of matter and energy. The scientific method, by contrast, examines cause-and-effect relationships through experimentation, drawing conclusions through observation and repeatability. Science operates under the assumption that the world of matter and energy behaves in a consistent manner, but it does not address the philosophical questions of whether any reality lies outside of this material world and whether normal patterns of nature are ever interrupted by a new causal agent, a supernatural force or being.

Miracles are therefore outside the realm of strict scientific investigation. The question of miracles must be addressed first philosophically, as to their possibility, and then historically, as to their actual occurrence.

PHILOSOPHICAL OBJECTIONS TO MIRACLES

Perhaps the most influential philosophical opposition to the miraculous came from eighteenth-century Scottish philosopher David Hume. Hume's primary argument was that human experience confirms the certainty and inviolability of the laws of nature. Since miracles are by definition violations of these laws, it would take an overwhelming amount of evidence—an impossibly high standard of proof—to confirm any miracle. Belief in miracles is therefore irrational.

A serious problem with Hume's argument is that it assumes *a priori* that the laws of nature are inviolable. But these so-called laws are really observations and hypotheses of how energy and matter work. As science has advanced, many supposedly inviolable laws have been radically modified and revised. Much that happens in the universe is beyond our expectations or present understanding. Furthermore, nothing in Hume's argument rules out the intervention of a god to alter the expected pattern of nature.

MIRACLES AND THE HISTORICAL METHOD

While the study of miracles is outside the realm of strict scientific investigation, it is not outside the realm of historical research, which depends on the written and oral reports of those who witnessed past events. The historian's role is to find out what happened, not to assume what could or could not have happened. Which is more historically objective, to assume miracles cannot occur or to keep an open but cautious perspective? Judging by personal experience, we might say miracles are uncommon and outside the realm of normalcy, but we cannot rule in advance that they are impossible. A miracle should be believed if there is enough historical evidence to confirm it with a high degree of probability.

DID JESUS PERFORM MIRACLES?

There is nearly universal agreement today—among liberals and conservatives alike—that Jesus was viewed by his contemporaries as a healer and an exorcist. The Gospel tradition is permeated with the miraculous. Rationalistic quests for the historical Jesus sometimes claimed that the miracle stories were developed by the church as it gradually deified Jesus, transforming him from a human teacher to the powerful Son of God. Yet peeling away the supernatural to find a nonmiraculous core of Gospel tradition is like peeling an onion. When the last peel is removed, nothing is left to study. Miracles appear in all strata of the Gospel tradition. References to Jesus' miracles also appear in a variety of Gospel genres, including miracle stories, pronouncement stories, controversy stories, sayings, parables, commissioning accounts, passion narratives, and summaries of Jesus' activities.

Jewish sources outside of the New Testament also refer to Jesus' miracles. Josephus states that Jesus was "a doer of startling deeds" (*Ant.* 18.3.3 §63), a probable reference to his miracles. The Babylonian Talmud claims Jesus was executed because he practiced magic and led Israel astray (*b. Sanh.* 43a). While this passage is a strong polemic against Jesus and Christianity, it admits as reliable the tradition that Jesus performed supernatural acts. The early church leader Origen quotes his second-century pagan opponent Celsus as claiming that Jesus worked certain magical powers which he had learned in Egypt (*Contra Celsus* 1:38).

While this data does not prove that Jesus performed miracles, it confirms that he was widely acclaimed as a miracle worker—even among his enemies. The question of whether Jesus performed specific miracles must be judged on a case-by-case basis. In most episodes, there is little information outside of the account itself by which to judge it. Much therefore depends on one's attitude toward and approach to the Gospels. If we assume miracles are impossible, then the account will of course be rejected. If we affirm that miracles are possible and that Jesus was an exceptional person viewed by his contemporaries as a miracle worker, then it is reasonable to conclude that the event took place.

THE SIGNIFICANCE OF JESUS' MIRACLES: THE POWER AND PRESENCE OF THE KINGDOM

The Synoptic Gospels draw a close connection between Jesus' proclamation of the kingdom of God and his miracles. The exorcisms and healings are intended to reveal the presence and power of the kingdom in Jesus' ministry.

Exorcisms. As we've noted, it is widely accepted that Jesus was recognized by his contemporaries as an exorcist. What significance, then, did Jesus give to his exorcisms? The evidence suggests that he viewed them as a spiritual assault on the dominion of Satan by the kingdom of God. This theme appears most clearly in the Beelzebul controversy (Mark 3:22–27; Matt. 12:22–30; Luke 11:14–15, 17–23). When the Pharisees accuse Jesus of casting out demons by the power of Beelzebul (Satan), Jesus first refutes the charge by noting how foolish it would be for Satan to cast out his own demons. He then offers an alternative explanation: "But if it is by the Spirit of God that I drive out demons, then the kingdom of God has come upon you" (Matt. 12:28; cf. Luke 11:20). In Jesus' exorcisms, the kingdom of God is manifested through the defeat of Satan. Jesus then offers an analogy: Satan is like a strong man trying to protect his estate, but Jesus is a stronger man who attacks and plunders Satan's property. Through his exorcisms, Jesus is attacking Satan's realm and taking back Satan's "possessions," those people over whom Satan has gained control. The exorcisms are proof that the kingdom of God is engaging and overwhelming the kingdom of Satan.

Healings. Like the exorcisms, Jesus' healings are closely associated with his kingdom announcement. This comes out most clearly in the question asked by John the Baptist (Luke 7:18–23; Matt. 11:2–6). John, imprisoned by Herod Antipas, sends his disciples to ask whether Jesus is indeed "the one who is to come" (the Messiah). Jesus' response illuminates the significance of his healing miracles: "Go back and report to John what you have seen and heard: The blind receive sight, the lame walk, those who have leprosy are cleansed, the deaf hear, the dead are raised, and the good news is proclaimed to the poor" (Luke 7:22; cf. Matt. 11:4–5). Jesus is here alluding to passages from Isaiah that predict God's final salvation—the messianic age—when evil will be defeated and the effects of sin and the fall of humanity will be reversed (Isa. 26:19; 29:18–19; 35:5–6; 61:1–2). Jesus' healing miracles are evidence of the coming of the kingdom, a foretaste of the restoration of creation promised in Isaiah and the prophets. Just as Adam's fall brought sickness and death, so Jesus' coming will bring healing and life.

Raising the Dead. The most dramatic of Jesus' healings are the three occasions he raises people from the dead: Jairus's daughter (Mark 5:21–43 par.), the widow's son (Luke 7:11–17), and Lazarus (John 11). There is also the allusion to Isaiah 26:19 in Jesus' response to John: "the dead are raised" (Luke 7:22; Matt. 11:5). While sometimes called "resurrections," these are better termed *resuscitations* or *revivifications*, since they restore normal mortal life rather than immortal resurrection life. In Jewish and Christian thought, resurrection occurs at the end of time, when believers receive glorified and immortal bodies. According to Paul, Jesus' own resurrection was the "firstfruits"—the beginning and guarantee—of this end-times resurrection (1 Cor. 15:20; cf. Col. 1:18).

Jesus' answer to John, with its allusion to Isaiah 26:19 ("the dead are raised"), indicates that the significance of these resuscitations is the same as that of the other healings: they symbolically inaugurate the kingdom of God and the new creation. The revivifications provide a preview and foretaste of the final resurrection and the consummation of the kingdom.

Nature Miracles. Perhaps the most difficult miracles for modern skeptics to accept are those in which Jesus demonstrates authority over the forces of nature—turning water into wine, multiplying loaves and fishes, withering a fig tree with a command, walking on the water, and calming the storm. For many, these feats seem more like the arbitrary actions of the Greek gods than the in-breaking power of the kingdom of God. Yet these nature miracles have striking parallels with Jesus' parables and function like enacted parables. As the parables reveal the mystery of the kingdom to those with ears to hear, so the nature miracles demonstrate the power and nature of the kingdom to those with eyes to see.

An example of the symbolic significance of these miracles is Jesus' withering of the fig tree upon his entrance to Jerusalem (Mark 11:12–14, 20–25; Matt. 21:18–22). The story is not a petty outburst of temper, as some have supposed, but an enacted parable. In the Old Testament, Israel is often compared to a fig tree or an unfruitful vineyard which God will judge. This imagery is taken up elsewhere by Jesus in a parable of an unfruitful fig tree (Luke 13:6–9). The fig tree in the parable and the fig tree which Jesus withers outside Jerusalem both represent the leaders of Israel, who face God's judgment if they fail to repent at Jesus' kingdom proclamation.

Another example of an enacted parable is Jesus' turning water to wine at the wedding in Cana of Galilee (John 2:1–11). While at first sight the miracle seems like a kind gesture to avoid embarrassment for the bridal party, in fact it carries rich symbolic significance. Elsewhere, Jesus tells a parable about the danger of putting new wine in old wineskins. When the new wine ferments and expands, it will burst the old wineskin (Mark 2:18–22). The meaning of the parable is that the "new wine" of the kingdom of God is a radical new thing which God is accomplishing. It cannot simply be poured into the old wineskins of Judaism. It is noteworthy that the jars at Cana are said to be "the kind used by the Jews for ceremonial washing" (John 2:6). The "water" of Jewish legalism is transformed into the new "wine" of the kingdom.

CONCLUSION

The question of Jesus' miracles is first of all a philosophical one (Are miracles possible?) and second a historical one (Is there sufficient evidence to accept as reliable specific miracle stories?). If miracles are not ruled out in advance, the accounts of Jesus' miracles fare well under critical scrutiny. They are widely attested to in a range of Gospel sources and forms, and they cohere well with the almost certainly authentic preaching of Jesus about the kingdom.

For Jesus, the miracles are not showy demonstrations of power or even proof of his identity. They are rather manifestations of the in-breaking power of the kingdom of God, a foretaste and preview of the restoration of creation promised by God through the prophets of old, now coming to fulfillment through Jesus the Messiah.

Questions for Review and Discussion

1. In what ways is the question of miracles both a philosophical one and a historical one?
2. Why do most historians accept that Jesus had a reputation as a healer and exorcist? What is the evidence for this?

3. According to Jesus' own teaching, what was the significance of his exorcisms? His healings? The revivifications? The nature miracles?

Recommended Resources

Brown, Colin. *Miracles and the Critical Mind.* Grand Rapids: Eerdmans, 1984.

Keener, Craig. *Miracles: The Credibility of the New Testament Accounts.* Grand Rapids: Baker, 2011.

Twelftree, Graham H. *Jesus the Miracle Worker: A Historical and Theological Study.* Downers Grove, IL: InterVarsity, 1999.

Wenham, David, and Craig Blomberg, eds. *The Miracles of Jesus.* Gospel Perspectives, vol. 6. Sheffield: JSOT, 1986.

CHAPTER 17

JESUS' MESSIANIC WORDS AND ACTIONS

Jesus' preaching about the kingdom, and his reputation as a miracle worker, raise the critical question of how he understood his identity and mission. While our limited sources do not allow us to build a psychological profile of Jesus, the implicit significance of Jesus' words and deeds can tell us a great deal about how he viewed himself in relation to the nation of Israel and her scriptural heritage. In this chapter, we will look at some of the most widely acknowledged actions and teachings of Jesus in order to discern his mission and goals.

THE AUTHORITY OF JESUS

Announcing and Inaugurating the Kingdom of God. As we have seen, one of the most undisputed facts about the historical Jesus was his announcement of the kingdom of God. The significance of this message must not be underestimated. Jesus claimed to be the agent of God's final salvation, bringing restoration to Israel, and healing and wholeness to the world. Even if we leave off the question of whether Jesus considered himself in any sense divine, his claim of authority to announce and establish the kingdom of God was truly an audacious one.

Authority over Demons and Disease. The significance Jesus gave to his healings and exorcisms reinforced his claim to be the inaugurator of God's kingdom. While healers and exorcists were not unknown in the ancient world, Jesus was unique in connecting his healings and exorcisms to the in-breaking power of God's reign. If his exorcisms were the work of God, "then the kingdom of God has come upon

130

you" (Matt. 12:28; Luke 11:20). The healings were evidence that Isaiah's signs of the eschatological salvation were being fulfilled in Jesus' ministry (Luke 7:22–23; Matt. 11:4–5).

Authority over the Law and the Sabbath. This sense of personal authority comes through especially in Jesus' attitude toward the law and in his declarations about the Sabbath. We have already seen that Jesus expressed unprecedented authority to expand, interpret, and fulfill the law for the new age of salvation (Matt. 5:17–48).

This same sense of authority is seen in the Sabbath controversies (Mark 2:23–28 par.; 3:1–6 par.; Luke 13:10–17; 14:1–6; John 5:2–18; 9:1–41). When the Pharisees accuse Jesus' disciples of violating the Sabbath, Jesus points out that meeting human needs represents the true essence of the Sabbath: "The Sabbath was made for man, not man for the Sabbath" (Mark 2:27). Yet Jesus then goes further and concludes that he himself is Lord of the Sabbath (Mark 2:28). Similarly, in John's Gospel, Jesus is accused of breaking the Sabbath when he heals a lame man at the Pool of Bethesda (John 5:16–18). Jesus responds by comparing his actions to God's ("my Father"), who also works on the Sabbath to sustain creation. The analogy infuriates his opponents, who plot to kill Jesus because "he was even calling God his own Father, making himself equal with God."

Again, the significance of Jesus' claims about the law and the Sabbath must not be understated. They go beyond the words and actions of a prophet who merely speaks for God. Jesus places himself in authority over the law and does so on the basis of his role in salvation history.

Authority to Forgive Sins. Another extraordinary claim by Jesus is his authority to forgive sins (Mark 2:1–12 par.; Luke 7:36–50). Some have argued that this claim is not so profound, since Jesus is merely acting as God's agent, offering his forgiveness. It should first be noted that this is not how the Gospel writers understood it, since they present Jesus' audience as shocked and indignant at Jesus' claims: "He's blaspheming! Who can forgive sins but God alone?" (Mark 2:7). From the perspective of his hearers, Jesus is claiming a prerogative of God.

Even if we suppose that Jesus is acting merely as God's agent, the claim to forgive sins is extraordinary when placed in the context of

Jesus' kingdom preaching. The prophet Jeremiah promised an eschatological new covenant, when God would provide full forgiveness of sins (Jer. 31:31–34). Jesus' offer of forgiveness is evidence that he is inaugurating the new covenant between God and his people. And this new covenant is inextricably connected to the coming of the kingdom of God (Luke 22:20, 29–30).

Authority at the Final Judgment. One of the most astonishing claims made by Jesus was that the destiny of human beings depended on their response to him. In Matthew 10:32–33, Jesus says, "Whoever acknowledges me before others, I will also acknowledge before my Father in heaven. But whoever disowns me before others, I will disown before my Father in heaven" (cf. Luke 12:8–9; Mark 8:35–38 par.; 9:37; Matt. 10:40). The Old Testament portrays God alone as the judge of the whole world (Pss. 9:8; 50:6; 82:8; 94:2; 96:13; 98:9; Isa. 2:4). Yet Jesus claims the prerogative to act as final judge (cf. Matt. 25:31–46).

THE AIMS OF JESUS

Closely related to Jesus' authority is the question of what he was trying to accomplish. Here we will deal with evidence that Jesus intended to establish a new community of faith, the eschatological people of God. In the next chapter, we will examine how this aim was related to predictions concerning his death.

Calling Disciples: A New Community of Faith. One of the most undisputed aspects of Jesus' ministry is his call of disciples to follow him (Matt. 4:18–22; Mark 1:16–20). Discipleship was common in Jesus' day, both in Judaism and in the broader Hellenistic world, and students would often seek out and attach themselves to a respected rabbi or philosopher. Jesus appears to have been unique in actively seeking out and calling his disciples. Also unique was the commitment he demanded of them (Mark 8:34–35 par.; Matt. 10:37–39 par.; John 12:25).

While Jesus had many followers, the Gospels agree that he chose twelve "apostles" to form a unique group (Mark 3:13–19; Matt. 10:1–4; Luke 6:12–16; John 6:67, 70; 20:24; cf. 1 Cor. 15:5). In its Jewish context, the number twelve was profoundly meaningful, signifying the twelve tribes of Israel. Jesus himself made this connection at the Last Supper, when he told the Twelve that in his kingdom they would sit on twelve thrones, judging the tribes of Israel (Luke 22:30; Matt. 19:28). Jesus certainly viewed this new community of followers as the righteous remnant of Israel—the reconstituted people of God.

This conclusion fits well the context of first-century Judaism, in which other groups, like the sectarians at Qumran, viewed themselves as the authentic remnant of Israel. It also fits well with Jesus' preaching of the kingdom. The twelve tribes had not existed as a united kingdom since the glorious days of King David and his son Solomon. While many Jews had returned from Babylonian exile to reconstitute the nation, the motley band of returnees under Persian rule did not fit the glorious and triumphant restoration—led by Yahweh himself!—that was predicted in the Prophets (Isaiah 40). Many Jews longed for the day when God would bring about a new exodus, a true return from exile to reunify and restore the tribes of Israel (Isa. 11:10–16; 49:6; Ezek. 45:8; 47:13; Mic. 2:12; Sir. 48:10; *Psalms of Solomon* 17:28). This hope was often linked to the coming reign of the LORD's anointed, the Messiah from the line of David (Isa. 11:1–16; Jer. 23:5–8; Hos. 3:5; *Pss. Sol.* 17–18; 4 Ezra 13). Jesus' choice of the Twelve, together with his preaching about the kingdom, confirms that he saw his mission as the restoration of Israel. It is also important to note that Jesus did not count himself as one of the Twelve. He was fulfilling the role of Yahweh himself, who called Israel into existence.

Dining with Sinners: The Universal Offer of the Kingdom. Another aspect of Jesus' ministry that is both unique and undisputed historically is his frequent association with sinners and outcasts of society. Jesus had a reputation for being "a friend of tax collectors and sinners" (Luke 7:34; Matt. 11:19).

The call of Levi illustrates this (Mark 2:13–17; Luke 5:27–32; cf. Matt. 9:9–13). Jesus shocks the religious leaders by calling a despised tax collector to be his disciple and attending a banquet in Levi's home. Appalled, the Pharisees and scribes demand from Jesus' disciples, "Why does he eat with tax collectors and sinners?" (Mark 2:16). Table fellowship had great significance in the ancient world and meant social acceptance of those with whom you dined.

Jesus responds, "It is not the healthy who need a doctor, but the sick. I have not come to call the righteous, but sinners to repentance" (Luke 5:31–32). The Great Physician came to heal not the self-righteous but sinners who recognize their need of spiritual healing.

Jesus' words and actions demonstrate something new and revolutionary about the kingdom of God. No longer is fellowship with God the exclusive right of priests and the religious elite. The new age of salvation means free forgiveness of sins to all who respond in faith. Throughout the Gospels, Jesus' teaching and parables reflect this great paradox and reversal. The proud and self-righteous reject the kingdom and are rejected. Sinners and outcasts joyfully repent and receive the kingdom.

Jesus and the Gentiles: Salvation for All Humanity. Most remarkable is Jesus' attitude toward the ultimate outsiders, from Israel's perspective—the Gentiles. It seems clear that Jesus at first directed his ministry only to Jews. When he commissions the Twelve, he tells them to go only to "the lost sheep of Israel" (Matt. 10:6). And at first, he refuses to exorcize a Gentile woman's daughter, saying, "I was sent only to the lost sheep of Israel" (Matt. 15:24). Jesus clearly viewed the gospel message as first for the Jews (cf. Rom. 1:16). This fits Jesus' proclamation of the kingdom of God, which in the Old Testament would be inseparable from Israel's calling as a nation. It also fits Jesus' appointment of the Twelve, the righteous remnant within Israel.

Yet Jesus repeatedly hints that his message of salvation is a universal one that will ultimately go to all people everywhere. When he heals the servant of a Roman centurion, Jesus marvels that "I have not found such great faith even in Israel" (Luke 7:1–10; Matt. 8:5–13). He then predicts that many outsiders will come from east, west, north, and south for the feast in the kingdom of God, while many in Israel will be cast out (Matt. 8:11–12; cf. Luke 13:28–29). The messianic banquet will be not for Israel alone but for all those who respond in faith.

This theme too fits the Old Testament background. The age of salvation is portrayed by the prophets as a time when all nations will go to Jerusalem to worship the LORD (Isa. 2:2–3). This theme took two distinct streams in Judaism. In one stream, the Gentiles are depicted as subject to Israel, coming to Jerusalem as vassals to pay tribute and to recognize the LORD's sovereignty. The other stream—and the one with which Jesus identified—affirms not the subjection of the nations but their salvation. Israel's glorious restoration will bring a "light for revelation" to the Gentiles (Luke 2:32). All humanity will experience God's salvation (Isa. 42:6; 49:6; Luke 2:32; Acts 13:47). In fulfillment of Israel's mission, Jesus now calls out a righteous remnant from within Israel to proclaim God's salvation to all nations (Luke 24:46–48; Acts 1:8; Matt. 28:16–20).

The Triumphal Entry. As Jesus' general actions of calling disciples and dining with sinners have symbolic significance with reference to his aims and intentions, so also do specific actions like entering Jerusalem on a colt (Mark 11:1–10; Matt. 21:1–9; Luke 19:28–40; John 12:12–19) and clearing the temple of money changers (see next section).

Pilgrims coming to Jerusalem for one of the festivals would normally approach the city on foot. Yet Jesus sends his disciples to procure a young donkey, one which has never been ridden before. The scene is particularly striking since Jesus is never depicted elsewhere in the Gospels as riding an animal. Why here? The most likely answer is that Jesus is intentionally enacting Zechariah 9:9: "Rejoice greatly, Daughter Zion! . . . See, your king comes to you, righteous and victorious, lowly and riding on a donkey, on a colt, the foal of a donkey."

Some scholars have claimed that the Gospel story is a legend created by the early church to portray Jesus as the Messiah. Yet this is unlikely for various reasons. First, Mark's version, presumably the earliest, does not explicitly refer to Zechariah 9:9. If the story were created around this prophecy, we might expect Mark (and Luke) to quote it. Second, the cry of the crowd, "Hosanna! Blessed is he who comes in the name of the Lord!" (Mark 11:9), has the mark of authenticity. These words allude to Psalm 118 (v. 26), a common psalm of pilgrims coming to Jerusalem for the feasts of Tabernacles and Passover. *Hosanna* is a Hebrew word meaning "save now." It is unlikely that the Greek-speaking church would have invented a saying that uses a Hebrew term and which only opaquely refers to Jesus' messianic identity.

If the episode was intentionally enacted by Jesus, what does it mean? Like the cursing of the fig tree and the clearing of the temple, it seems to be both an act of self-revelation and a provocation. Jesus symbolically announces his messianic claim and challenges Israel's leaders to respond. His identification with Zechariah 9:9 also tells us something about his messianic consciousness. Jesus enters the city not riding a warhorse, ready for battle against the Romans, but rather as the humble, peace-bringing king. He will bring salvation not through physical conquest but through self-sacrificial service.

Clearing the Temple. A second episode, even more widely accepted as authentic among scholars, is Jesus' "cleansing," or clearing, of the temple (Mark 11:12–17; Matt. 21:12–21; Luke 19:45–46; cf. John 2:13–17). Jesus enters the temple, driving out those who are selling animals for sacrifices, and overturning the tables of the money changers. Almost all scholars today agree (1) that Jesus performed some kind of symbolic action in the temple, and (2) that it was this action that prompted Jesus' opponents to act against him (see Mark 11:18; Luke 19:47).

Jesus' actions are often identified as a cleansing to remove defilement. This would follow the model of the Maccabees, who purified and rededicated the temple after it was defiled by the pagan sacrifices of Antiochus Epiphanes (see chapter 2). Jesus restores the temple once again to "a house of prayer for all nations" (Mark 11:17).

Yet while Jesus' actions were certainly a purging, there seems more to the event than this. In both Matthew and Mark, the incident is closely related to Jesus' cursing of the fig tree. This latter event is almost certainly a symbolic act of judgment against Israel. Elsewhere, Jesus repeatedly predicts the coming judgment and destruction of Jerusalem and the temple (Mark 13:2 par.; 14:58 par.; 15:29 par.; Luke 13:34–35; 19:41–44; cf. John 2:19–21). It seems likely therefore that Jesus' actions in the temple were not only a cleansing but a symbolic act of judgment, an enacted parable of its destruction.

Some scholars claim that Jesus envisioned not only the destruction of the temple but also its restoration. There is a tradition in Judaism that the coming Messiah would restore and rebuild the temple to be more glorious than ever (2 Sam. 7:13; Zech. 6:13; Mal. 3:1). While this interpretation is possible, more likely Jesus saw the temple's permanent replacement as a part of the dawning of the new age. In the new age of salvation, forgiveness of sins would come no longer through the temple and its sacrificial system but through Jesus' sacrifice on the cross, the temple of his body, destroyed and rebuilt through death and resurrection (John 2:19, 21). As Jesus tells the Samaritan woman, in the days to come, God's people would worship him "neither on this mountain [Mount Gerizim] nor in Jerusalem" but "in the Spirit and in truth" (John 4:21–24).

Questions for Review and Discussion

1. What claims did Jesus make that exhibit his extraordinary sense of authority?
2. What do the following features of Jesus' ministry indicate about his aims or purpose?
   a. His appointment of the Twelve
   b. His association with sinners and outcasts
   c. His attitude toward the Gentiles
   d. His entrance into Jerusalem on a donkey
   e. His clearing of the temple

Recommended Resources

Marshall, I. H. *The Origins of New Testament Christology.* Downers Grove, IL: InterVarsity, 1976.

Meyer, Ben F. *The Aims of Jesus.* London: SCM, 1979.

Witherington III, Ben. *The Christology of Jesus.* Minneapolis: Fortress, 1990.

Wright, N. T. *Jesus and the Victory of God.* Minneapolis: Fortress, 1996.

CHAPTER 18

JESUS' DEATH

HISTORICAL CIRCUMSTANCES OF THE DEATH OF JESUS

Much of the scholarly discussion about the circumstances of Jesus' death relates to the question of who was responsible for his arrest and crucifixion. Historically, the primary responsibility has been placed on the Jews. Throughout the centuries, this has sometimes had tragic consequences, resulting in anti-Semitism and violence against Jews. More recent trends in scholarship have shifted the blame to the Romans. The tendency to blame the Jews, it is said, arose in the decades after the crucifixion with the church's growing conflict with the synagogue and its desire to convince Rome that Christianity was no threat to the empire.

Most contemporary scholars recognize that there is not an either-or answer to this question but that both Jewish and Roman authorities must have played some role in Jesus' death.

Pilate and the Romans. The evidence points to the conclusion that Jesus was executed by the Romans for sedition—rebellion against the government. First, he was crucified as "king of the Jews." The *titulus* on the cross announcing this charge is widely regarded as historical (Mark 15:26 par.). Second, he was crucified between two "rebels," or "criminals"—Roman terms used of insurrectionists (Mark 15:27 par.). Another insurrectionist, Barabbas, was released in his place (Mark 15:6–13 par.).

While this evidence confirms the likely charge against Jesus, it raises the mystifying question of why Jesus was crucified, since he had almost nothing in common with other rebels and insurrectionists. He advocated love for enemies and commanded his followers to respond to persecution with acts of kindness (Matt. 5:38–48; Luke 6:27–36). He affirmed the legitimacy of paying taxes to Caesar (Mark 12:14,

17 par.). At his arrest, he ordered his disciples not to fight but to put away their swords (Matt. 26:52; Luke 22:49–51).

Why, then, did Pilate have Jesus crucified? While it is unlikely that Pilate viewed Jesus as a significant threat, he also had little interest in justice or compassion. We know from other sources that Pilate's governorship was characterized by a general disdain toward his Jewish subjects and by brutal suppression of opposition. At the same time, his support from Rome was shaky at best, and he feared antagonizing the Jewish leadership lest they complain to the emperor.

The portrait of Pilate we get from Roman and Jewish sources is remarkably similar to that of the Gospels—an unscrupulous and self-seeking leader who loathed the Jewish leadership but feared antagonizing them. When the Jewish leaders warned Pilate, "If you let this man go, you are no friend of Caesar" (John 19:12), he would surely have felt both anger and fear. Most likely, Pilate ordered Jesus' execution because (1) it placated the Jewish leaders and so headed off accusations against him to Rome, (2) it preemptively eliminated any threat Jesus might pose if the people actually tried to make him a king, and (3) it ruthlessly warned other would-be prophets and messiahs that Rome would stand for no dissent.

Jewish Opposition. During Jesus' Galilean ministry, he faced opposition primarily from the Pharisees and the scribes, centered especially on his teaching and actions relating to the law and the Sabbath. He claimed authority over the law, treated the Sabbath command as secondary to human needs, and accused the Pharisees of elevating their traditions over the commands of God. He also accused them of pride, hypocrisy, and greed, warning the people to do as they say but not as they do (Matt. 23:3). These actions certainly did not win him friends among the religious leaders.

While Jesus certainly made enemies before his final journey to Jerusalem, it was the events of the final week that resulted in his crucifixion. His primary opponents in Jerusalem were the priestly leadership, the Sanhedrin, and the Sadducees. As we noted in the previous chapter, Jesus' clearing of the temple is widely recognized as the key episode that provoked the Jewish authorities to act against him.

In Mark's account of Jesus' Jewish trial, false witnesses are brought forward who testify, "We heard him say, 'I will destroy this temple made with human hands and in three days will build another, not made with hands'" (14:58). The high priest then questions him: "Are you the Messiah, the Son of the Blessed One?" (v. 61), to which Jesus' replies, "I am. . . . And you will see the Son of Man sitting at the right hand of the Mighty One and coming on the clouds of heaven" (v. 62). The high priest responds with rage and accuses Jesus of blasphemy. The whole assembly calls for his death (Mark 14:57–65; cf. Matt. 26:55–68; Luke 22:66–71).

While some have questioned the historicity of this scene, it makes good sense when viewed in the context of Jesus' ministry. Jesus' temple action would naturally have prompted the high priest to ask if he was making a messianic claim. Jesus' response combines two key Old Testament passages, Psalm 110:1 and Daniel 7:13. The first indicates that Jesus will be vindicated by God and exalted to a position at his right hand. The latter suggests Jesus will receive sovereign authority to judge the enemies of God. By combining these verses, Jesus asserts that the Sanhedrin is acting against the LORD's anointed, that they will face judgment for this, and that Jesus himself will be their judge! Such an outrageous claim was blasphemous to the Sanhedrin, who viewed themselves as God's appointed leadership, the guardians of his holy temple. Jesus was challenging not only their actions but also their authority and legitimacy. Such a challenge demanded a response.

There were also political and social consequences to consider. Jesus' actions in the temple—probably viewed by the Sanhedrin as an act of sacrilege—together with his popularity among the people, made it imperative to act against him quickly and decisively. A disturbance of the peace might bring Roman retribution and disaster to the nation and its leaders (cf. John 11:48). The Sanhedrin therefore turned Jesus over to Pilate, modifying their religious charges to political ones—sedition and claiming to be a king in opposition to Caesar—and gained from Pilate a capital sentence.

JESUS' PERSPECTIVE ON HIS COMING DEATH

We turn from the external factors that provoked Jesus' death to his own perspective and intention. Did Jesus expect to die? Did he intend to? If so, how did he view his death?

Did Jesus Foresee His Death? According to the Synoptic Gospels, from Peter's confession at Caesarea Philippi onward, Jesus warned his disciples of his impending fate. Three times he predicts his suffering and death (Mark 8:31–32 par.; 9:31 par.; 10:33–34 par.). Some have argued that these passion predictions were prophecies created after the fact by the church, since Jesus could not have predicted his own death. Yet there is good evidence for their historicity: (1) Jesus uses the title Son of Man, which is characteristic of the historical Jesus rather than the later church; (2) there is no reference to the cross in these sayings; (3) there is no atonement theology expressed in them. Surely if the church invented these sayings, they would have included the manner and significance of Jesus' death.

Yet even from a merely human perspective, Jesus could have foreseen his fate. He faced constant opposition from the Pharisees and scribes, who considered him to be an agent of Satan (Mark 3:22–27), a blasphemer (Mark 2:7), and a Sabbath breaker (Mark 2:23–28; 3:1–6; Luke 13:10–17; 14:1–6; John 5:1–18; 7:19–24). He must have known that they wished to get rid of him.

Jesus the Suffering Prophet. In the same vein, Jesus often spoke of the persecution and murder of the Old Testament prophets and identified himself with them (Mark 6:4; Matt. 13:57; Luke 4:24; cf. Mark 12:1–11 par.; Matt. 5:12; 13:57; 23:29–39; Luke 6:23, 26; 11:47–50; 13:33–35). The early church is unlikely to have created these "prophet" sayings, preferring exalted titles for Jesus like Messiah, Son of God, and Lord. It is safe to conclude that Jesus viewed himself as a prophet and expected the fate that befell the prophets—persecution and even death.

THE SIGNIFICANCE OF JESUS' DEATH

If Jesus expected his own death, what significance did he give to it? The most important evidence for this comes from two key passages: the words and actions of Jesus at the Last Supper, and the ransom saying in Mark 10:45.

The Last Supper. The eucharistic words of Jesus have a strong claim to authenticity (Mark 14:23–24; Matt. 26:26–29; Luke 22:15–20; 1 Cor. 11:23–26). In about AD 55, Paul wrote to the church in

Corinth, "I received from the Lord what I also passed on to you: The Lord Jesus, on the night he was betrayed, took bread, and when he had given thanks, he broke it and said, 'This is my body, which is for you; do this in remembrance of me.' In the same way, after supper he took the cup, saying, 'This cup is the new covenant in my blood; do this, whenever you drink it, in remembrance of me'" (1 Cor. 11:23–25).

Paul claims to have received this tradition from those who were believers before him. Since Paul's conversion occurred just a few years after Jesus' death, around AD 35, this eucharistic tradition must be very early.

The significance of Jesus' words is to be found in four closely related Jewish symbols: Passover, exodus, sacrifice, and covenant. The Synoptics explicitly identify the Last Supper as a Passover meal, and there is strong evidence to support this. Like the Passover, the Last Supper was eaten at night (the normal daily meal was in the late afternoon), while reclining (ordinary meals were eaten sitting), and in the city of Jerusalem. Though Jesus was staying in Bethany, he came to Jerusalem since the Passover had to be eaten within the city limits. The meal ended with a hymn, presumably the *Hallel* psalms sung at the end of the Passover meal (Psalms 115–118; Mark 14:26; Matt. 26:30). Jesus acts as the traditional head of the household in explaining the meaning of the Passover. Yet Jesus' words confirm that this is no ordinary Passover but the establishment of a new Passover for the new age of salvation—the kingdom of God.

The original Passover represented God's greatest act of deliverance in the Hebrew Scriptures and the creation of Israel as a nation. With his mighty power, Yahweh delivered his people through the sacrificial blood of the Passover lamb and brought them out of slavery in Egypt. Jesus' eucharistic words recall and transform the rich symbols of Passover, announcing the arrival of the new exodus and a new covenant. The unleavened bread of the Passover meal represents Jesus' body, given for his disciples. The implication is that he is the new Passover lamb (cf. 1 Cor. 5:7). The Passover wine represents the blood of the new covenant. Jesus' words in Mark 14:24, "This is my blood of the covenant," echo Moses' words in Exodus 24:8, where Moses sprinkles the blood of the sacrifice on the people and says, "This is the blood of the covenant that the LORD has made with you."

In Luke 22:20 and 1 Corinthians 11:25, Jesus speaks explicitly of the *new* covenant, a clear allusion to Jeremiah 31 and the eschatological new covenant that will bring forgiveness of sins and personal knowledge of God (Jer. 31:31–34; cf. Zech. 9:9–11).

Jesus' words at the Last Supper thus fit well his preaching about the kingdom of God and the dawn of the new age. They also provide important clues as to how he viewed his approaching death. Jesus inaugurates a new Passover meal celebrating the new covenant and the arrival of the kingdom of God. While the first covenant was instituted with the blood of sacrificial animals, this new covenant will be established through his own blood. It seems likely therefore that Jesus viewed his death as a sacrifice of atonement, leading his people in a new exodus from bondage to sin and death.

Another Old Testament allusion in Jesus' eucharistic words takes us further toward Jesus' understanding of his death. Jesus speaks of "my blood of the covenant, which is poured out for many" (Mark 14:24; Matt. 26:28). The phrase "poured out for many" probably alludes to Isaiah 53:11–12, where the Servant of the LORD "will justify many" and "bore the sin of many." With these words, Jesus identifies himself as Isaiah's Suffering Servant and interprets his coming death as a sacrifice of atonement for the sins of his people.

The Ransom Saying. This self-understanding finds support in Jesus' words in Mark 10:45. After calling his disciples to a life of servant leadership (Mark 10:42–44), Jesus concludes, "Even the Son of Man did not come to be served, but to serve, and to give his life as a ransom for many" (10:45). The term "ransom" or "redemption" *(lytron)* means a price paid to free someone, like a slave or a prisoner of war. Jesus thus interprets his death as a substitutionary payment or sacrifice for his people.

The authenticity of the saying has been challenged by some scholars. It is argued that Jesus could not have spoken of his death in this forthright manner and that the saying reflects the church's later atonement theology. Yet the words have an Aramaic background which argues for their authenticity. Furthermore, we have pointed to strong evidence that Jesus not only viewed himself as the Messiah inaugurating the kingdom of God (chap. 15) but also expected to suffer and die (see previous section). Since everything else in Jesus' words and deeds points to his role as the culmination of Israel's history and Scriptures, we would expect him to understand his death in the same way.

The most likely background to Jesus' words in Mark 10:45 is found in the description of the Suffering Servant in Isaiah 53:11–12: "By his knowledge my righteous servant will justify many, and he will bear their iniquities. . . . He poured out his life unto death, and was numbered with the transgressors. . . . He bore the sin of many, and made intercession for the transgressors."

Jesus' identification of himself as a servant who offers himself as "a ransom for many" (Mark 10:45) strongly echoes this passage, suggesting that he saw his role as Isaiah's Servant of the LORD (cf. Mark 1:11; 14:24; Matt. 8:17; 12:15–21; Luke 4:16–21; 22:37; John 1:29, 36; 12:38).

We may conclude that it is likely that Jesus not only foresaw his death but moved to make it happen, interpreting it in light of the Suffering Servant of Isaiah 53—a sacrificial act of atonement for the sins of his people.

Questions for Review and Discussion

1. What role did the Roman authorities and the Jewish religious leaders likely play in the arrest, trial, and crucifixion of Jesus?
2. What is the evidence that Jesus foresaw and predicted his own death?
3. What significance did Jesus give to his death? What evidence is there for the historicity of Jesus' eucharistic words and of the ransom saying of Mark 10:45?

Recommended Resources

Brown, Raymond. *The Death of the Messiah: From Gethsemane to the Grave.* New York: Doubleday, 1994.

Jeremias, Joachim. *The Eucharistic Words of Jesus.* New Testament Library. London: SCM, 1966.

Marshall, I. H. *Last Supper and Lord's Supper.* Grand Rapids: Eerdmans, 1980.

CHAPTER 19

JESUS' RESURRECTION

Throughout the New Testament, the resurrection is viewed as *the vindication of the message and mission of Jesus.* If God raised Jesus from the dead, then his claims are true and the salvation he announced has been achieved. The apostle Paul affirmed that if the resurrection did not take place, Christianity is a false religion and should be abandoned: "If Christ has not been raised, our preaching is useless and so is your faith. More than that, we are then found to be false witnesses about God. . . . But Christ has indeed been raised from the dead, the firstfruits of those who have fallen asleep" (1 Cor. 15:14–20).

For Paul, the death and resurrection of Jesus was the turning point in human history, the transition from the age of promise to the age of fulfillment. If the resurrection took place, Christianity is true; if it didn't, Christianity is folly and Christians are only to be pitied. No event in human history has more riding on it than the resurrection.

RATIONALISTIC EXPLANATIONS FOR THE RESURRECTION

As with the other Gospel miracles, critics have sought to discount the resurrection through rationalistic explanations. A variety of alternatives to the physical resurrection of Jesus have been proposed.

The Swoon Theory. This is the view that Jesus never really died on the cross. He simply swooned, or fainted, and the soldiers assumed he was dead. He was placed in the tomb in a comatose state, where he revived. He escaped, appeared to his disciples, and subsequently died of his injuries.

This explanation stretches the limits of credibility and has been rightly rejected by critical scholars. The Romans were experts at crucifixion, and it is inconceivable that they would have botched the job. Even if Jesus were still alive when laid in the tomb, the chances are practically nil that he could recover from the severe trauma of crucifixion. Most damaging of all, it is inconceivable that a barely alive Jesus staggering into Jerusalem could have convinced his disciples that he had risen victoriously from the dead.

The Wrong Tomb Theory. This is the theory that on Easter morning, the women got confused concerning where Jesus was buried and came across an empty tomb. Excited by their discovery, they began proclaiming the resurrection.

This explanation is also highly unlikely. The Gospels report that the women carefully noted the location of the tomb in order to return later to anoint the body (Matt. 27:61; Mark 15:47; Luke 23:55). Could they have forgotten so quickly? We then have to suppose that everyone else also went to the wrong tomb, including Peter and John (John 20:2–10), Jesus' opponents, and even Joseph of Arimathea, who owned the tomb!

The Theft Theory. The claim that the disciples stole the body is the oldest rationalistic explanation for the resurrection, appearing already in Matthew's Gospel (Matt. 28:11–15). Yet this theory creates enormous problems both historically and ethically. Historically, all the evidence indicates that the disciples were emotionally devastated and discouraged following the crucifixion. There is little to indicate they expected a resurrection, much less plotted to fake one. Ethically, are we to believe that the same disciples who developed the greatest ethical system in the world and proclaimed the gospel as God's ultimate *truth* in fact propagated a great hoax and a lie?

The Visions and Legendary Development Theory. Few modern critical scholars hold to any of the previous three views. Almost all who deny the resurrection today claim that the resurrection accounts arose over time from dreams and visions of Jesus that the disciples began having after his death. These visions were probably first understood spiritually, as the church came to believe that Jesus had been vindicated by God and spiritually exalted to his right hand. In time, however, these visions grew into resurrection legends in which an empty tomb was discovered and Jesus' disciples saw him alive.

HISTORICAL EVIDENCE FOR THE RESURRECTION

How do we respond to this legendary development proposal? To do so, we must build a case from the ground up. While nothing can be proven historically with absolute certainty, some things have such strong evidential support that they can be confirmed beyond reasonable doubt. The following five points represent key corroborating evidence for the resurrection.

1. Jesus Was Crucified by the Romans around AD 30. No credible scholar today denies that Jesus existed or that he was crucified in Judea under orders from Pontius Pilate around AD 30. It is inconceivable, moreover, that Jesus did not die on the cross.

2. Jesus Was Buried in the Tomb of Joseph of Arimathea. All four Gospels affirm that Joseph of Arimathea, a member of the Sanhedrin, took the body of Jesus and buried it in his own tomb. It is highly unlikely that the church would have invented a story in which a member of the Sanhedrin—the council that condemned Jesus—performed such an action (Mark 14:55, 64; 15:1, 43). The burial of Jesus is confirmed in multiple sources: Matthew, Mark, Luke, John, Acts (2:31; 13:36–37), and the writing of Paul (1 Cor. 15:3–8). Significantly, Paul claims he received this tradition from believers before him. Paul was a first-generation Christian who personally knew Peter, James, and other believers in Jerusalem; thus his statement that Jesus "was buried" (1 Cor. 15:4) is confirmed beyond reasonable doubt.

3. The Tomb Was Discovered Empty on the Third Day. Just as the evidence that Jesus was buried is overwhelming, so also is the evidence that the tomb was discovered empty on the third day. First, all of the Gospels testify that *women* discovered the empty tomb. Since in first-century Judaism, women were not considered reliable witnesses, it is inconceivable that the church would invent such a story. Second, the claim that Jesus' body was stolen *presupposes* an empty tomb (Matt. 28:11–15). Matthew would have no reason to report this accusation unless it was actually circulating. Third, the very early testimony that Jesus rose on "the first day of the week" (Mark 16:2) indicates that a specific historical event prompted belief in the resurrection. Very early on, Christians began worshiping on the first day of the week, the Lord's Day. What could account for this change from the Sabbath (Saturday) to Sunday except the belief that Jesus arose on the Sunday after his crucifixion?

4. Many Credible Witnesses Saw Jesus Alive. Two pieces of evidence are particularly important here. First, there are the resurrection appearances to women. As just noted, these stories are unlikely to have been fabricated by the early church, since women were not viewed as reliable witnesses. Second, the very early primary-source account of Paul in 1 Corinthians 15:3–8 confirms that many people saw Jesus alive, including Peter, the Twelve, James the brother of Jesus, and more than five hundred others. Paul also notes that many of these were still alive, essentially challenging his critics to check out the reports for themselves.

There is no credible evidence that the disciples first had visions which later developed into resurrection accounts. A vision of Christ in heaven, such as that of Stephen at his martyrdom (Acts 7:56) or that of John in the book of Revelation (Rev. 1:12–16), is qualitatively different from an earthly encounter with the resurrected Jesus. Furthermore, legendary stories generally take time to develop, yet the church was proclaiming the bodily resurrection very soon after Jesus' death.

We must also ask, What could have sparked such visions? By all accounts, the disciples were not expecting Jesus to rise from the dead. When other messianic leaders were executed by the Romans, their followers dispersed. It would be pointless to begin proclaiming the leader's resurrection unless there was something to support it. It is also noteworthy that Jesus' brother James did not believe in him until after the resurrection (John 7:5; Mark 3:21). Something caused him to change his mind about Jesus.

A merely spiritual or visionary resurrection was also contrary to Jewish belief. According to the Pharisees—whose beliefs on this issue both Jesus and Paul shared—the resurrection was expected at the end of time, when the bodies of the righteous and the wicked would be raised (see the following discussion). Paul's whole point in 1 Corinthians 15 is the reality of bodily resurrection—the close link between the corruptible body that dies and the glorified body that rises (1 Cor. 15:42). It is inconceivable that Paul, a Jew with a Pharisaic background, would speak of the resurrection and mean a merely spiritual one.

5. The Lives of the Disciples Were Transformed. The fifth piece of verifiable evidence for the resurrection is the extraordinary change in the apostles. What else could account for the transformation of a small band of defeated disciples into a community of followers who could not be silenced by persecution or threat of martyrdom? Something happened on that Sunday morning that changed their lives, convincing them that Jesus was the risen and glorified Lord.

THE SIGNIFICANCE OF THE RESURRECTION

If the resurrection of Jesus can be verified with a high degree of probability, what did it mean in the context of Jesus' life and ministry? A theology of the resurrection is not well developed in the Old Testament. While a number of statements indicate resurrection life, or continuing existence in God's presence after death, only in Daniel 12 is the resurrection explicitly described: "Multitudes who sleep in the dust of the earth will awake: some to everlasting life, others to shame and everlasting contempt" (Dan. 12:2–3).

Jewish literature produced during the Second Temple period reveals an expanding theology of the resurrection. Most Jews of Jesus' day (the Sadducees were a notable exception) believed in the final resurrection, when God would raise the dead, reward the righteous, and judge the wicked. Both Jesus and Paul shared this perspective (Mark 12:18–27 par.; 1 Corinthians 15).

What, then, would the resurrection have meant for Jesus and his followers? Placing Jesus in his first-century Jewish context suggests two key answers.

1. The Beginning of the Last Days and the Final Resurrection. Jesus' resurrection went hand in hand with his preaching of the kingdom of God. The arrival of God's kingdom meant that the last days had begun and that God was about to intervene in human history to judge the righteous and the wicked. If, as we have argued, Jesus viewed his death as inaugurating the new covenant, his resurrection must be viewed as the beginning of the end-times resurrection of the people of God. This was not just the restoration of physical life but also glorification to a new mode of existence—the beginning of immortal, imperishable resurrection life (1 Cor. 15:50–56). As Paul puts it, Jesus is "the firstborn from among the dead" (Col. 1:18). His resurrection assures believers that they too will be raised in glorified bodies, shining "like the stars for ever and ever" (Dan. 12:3).

2. *The Defeat of Satan, Sin, and Death.* As the inaugurator of the kingdom, Jesus brings God's salvation. The resurrection confirms that Jesus' victory relates not merely to temporal enemies but to the evil spiritual forces of the world. Jesus' exorcisms confirm that he viewed his ministry as a conflict with Satan and the forces of evil. The nature of this battle is illuminated by Jesus' other actions: forgiving sins, healing the sick, and raising the dead. Jesus was battling not only Satan but also the power of sin, disease, and death.

When we place these conflicts in the context of Jesus' preaching of the kingdom of God, a coherent picture emerges. Jesus understood his death as an atoning sacrifice for the sins of his people, reversing the effects of the fall, defeating Satan (whose actions resulted in the fall), and restoring creation to its rightful relationship with God. In short, Jesus was restoring God's reign over creation. The resurrection demonstrated victory over death and marked the beginning of the end-times resurrection of the righteous.

To arrive at these extraordinary conclusions, we need not look centuries forward to the developed Christology of a later age; we look straight into the prophetic worldview of Jesus and his contemporaries, a worldview shaped by the restoration theology of Isaiah and the prophets. Isaiah predicted the coming age of salvation, a new exodus accomplished through the Davidic Messiah and the sacrificial ministry of the Servant of the LORD. Endowed with the Spirit of God, the Messiah would make atonement for the sins of his people, ushering in the eschatological year of the LORD's favor, when the lame would walk, the blind would see, the dead would rise. Death would be swallowed up in victory, and God would create a new heaven and a new earth (Isa. 2:1–4; 11:1–16; 25:8; 26:19; 29:18–19; 35:5–6; 52:13–53:12; 61:1–2; 65:17–18).

CONCLUSION

We may conclude our study of the historical Jesus by drawing together some of our results. In light of the extraordinary sense of destiny and authority exhibited by Jesus throughout the Gospel tradition, it seems likely that he considered himself the center of God's unfolding purpose for Israel and the world. He claimed—whether explicitly or implicitly—to be the Messiah, God's agent to accomplish salvation and to inaugurate the kingdom of God. He viewed his coming death through the lens of the restoration theology of Isaiah and the prophets: as an atoning sacrifice for the sins of his people, accomplishing a new exodus and establishing a new covenant bringing true forgiveness of sins and an intimate knowledge of God.

The evidence further suggests that Jesus did not remain in the tomb but rose alive on the third day, vindicating his claim to be the LORD's Messiah, God's agent of salvation for Israel and for the world. Reigning now at the right hand of God, he will one day return to bring salvation to his people and to judge the world.

With these last two conclusions, we are clearly crossing the always-fluid boundary between historical conclusions and faith confessions. It is impossible to read the Gospels and not play close to this line. The claims made by Jesus and by the Evangelists who interpreted him cannot be studied from a merely objective, neutral position. By its very nature, the gospel of Jesus Christ demands a response from the reader. Throughout the centuries, Christians have responded to this call for faith and have found meaning and purpose for living.

Questions for Review and Discussion

1. What is the most widely held rationalistic explanation today for the resurrection?
2. What are five pieces of highly reliable evidence that together support the historicity of the resurrection of Jesus?
3. How would Jesus have understood a theology of the resurrection in light of his Jewish background?

Recommended Resources

Craig, William Lane. *The Son Rises: The Historical Evidence for the Resurrection of Jesus.* Eugene, OR: Wipf and Stock, 2000.

Habermas, Gary, and Michael R. Licona. *The Case for the Resurrection of Jesus.* Grand Rapids: Kregel, 2004.

Licona, Michael R. *The Resurrection of Jesus: A New Historiographical Approach.* Downers Grove, IL: InterVarsity, 2010.

Wright, N. T. *The Resurrection of the Son of God.* Philadelphia: Fortress, 2003.

APPENDIX 1

HOW DID WE GET THE GOSPELS?

Source, Form, and Redaction Criticism

The Gospels did not simply fall from heaven. They were written by real authors to real churches within a variety of historical and cultural contexts in the first century. Examining the process by which the Gospels came to be can provide a better understanding of their nature and how they ought to be read and applied in the church today.

The Gospel story begins, of course, with the life of the historical Jesus. It is beyond dispute that Jesus of Nazareth was a historical figure who lived in Israel during the period of Roman domination and was crucified by the Roman governor Pontius Pilate sometime around 30–33. Nor is there any doubt that a short time after his death, his disciples came to believe that he had risen from the dead.

As the message of Jesus began to spread throughout the Roman Empire, stories about Jesus were told and retold, passed down by word of mouth. In time, these stories were put into written form. The writers of the Gospels took these written and oral sources and produced their works. From this brief overview, we can discern four main stages in the development of the Gospels.

Stage 1: The life, death, and resurrection of the historical Jesus
Stage 2: The period of oral tradition, when the sayings and stories of Jesus were passed down primarily through the spoken word
Stage 3: The period of written sources, when this oral material began to be written down
Stage 4: The writing of the Gospels themselves

Luke refers to these four stages in the introduction to his Gospel: "Many have undertaken to draw up an account of the things that have been fulfilled among us, just as they were handed down to us by those who from the first were eyewitnesses and servants of the word. With this in mind, since I myself have carefully investigated everything from the beginning, I too decided to write an orderly account for you, most excellent Theophilus, so that you may know the certainty of the things you have been taught" (Luke 1:1–4).

Notice that Luke speaks of the "things that have been fulfilled among us" (stage 1), the preaching of the "eyewitnesses and servants of the word" (stage 2), the "many" written accounts that had already been produced (stage 3), and Luke's writing of his own Gospel (stage 4).

Throughout the history of Gospel research, tools have been developed to examine each stage in this transmission process. These tools have become known as *historical criticism,* since they trace the history of the Jesus tradition through its various stages. The term *criticism* is used not in the sense of a negative assessment but in the sense of analysis or critique, as we might speak of a literary or film critic. The tools are:

Stage 1: Historical Jesus research examines the nature and historicity of the traditions about Jesus.

Stage 2: Form criticism attempts to identify and analyze how the stories about Jesus developed and were passed down orally (by word of mouth) in the church.

Stage 3: Source criticism tries to identify the written sources that lie behind the Gospels and their relationship to one another.

Stage 4: Redaction criticism seeks to determine how the Gospel writers edited, or "redacted," their sources to produce our present Gospels.

SOURCE CRITICISM AND THE SYNOPTIC PROBLEM

One of the first things any reader notices when reading through Matthew, Mark, and Luke is their striking similarity, especially in contrast to the Gospel of John. They tell many of the same stories and repeat much of Jesus' teaching. This naturally raises the question of their relationship. Why do these three so closely resemble each other? Why do they differ at so many points? While a small minority of scholars claim the Synoptics were written independently of one another, this seems unlikely. Even when two historians faithfully record the same event, they seldom use exactly the same words.

This suggests some kind of literary relationship. The question of this relationship is called the *synoptic problem*. Many source theories have been proposed, with each of the Synoptics suggested as the original. The most widely held view today is that Mark's Gospel was written first and that both Matthew and Luke used Mark. This is known as *Markan priority*.

Markan Priority. There is considerable evidence that Mark wrote first:

1. Though Matthew and Luke differ considerably from one another, more than 90 percent of Mark is found in one or the other. They seem to be using Mark as their common source.

2. In the "triple tradition" (stories included in all three Synoptics), readings in Matthew and Luke seldom agree with each other when one or the other differs from Mark.

3. Similarly, the order of events in Mark seems to be original. Whenever Matthew departs from Mark's order, Luke continues to follow Mark. The reverse is also true. Whenever Luke departs from Mark's order, Matthew continues to follow Mark.

4. Mark tends to have a rougher, less polished Greek style, which Matthew and Luke frequently smooth over.

5. Matthew and Luke tend to alter readings in Mark that could be taken as offensive. For example, Mark seems to limit Jesus' power in Nazareth when he writes that Jesus "could not do any miracles there" (Mark 6:5). Matthew avoids any possible misunderstanding by writing, "And he did not do many miracles there" (Matt. 13:58).

6. Mark occasionally preserves the original Aramaic words which Jesus used, such as *talitha koum* (5:41), *corban* (7:11), *ephphatha* (7:34), and *abba* (14:36). Matthew and Luke consistently replace these with a Greek translation. One would expect Mark's Aramaic words to be original.

These and other arguments have convinced most New Testament scholars that Mark was the first Gospel written.

Building on Markan Priority: The Two-Source Theory. The priority of Mark does not account for material that appears in both Matthew and Luke but not in Mark. This material is known as the "double tradition." To explain this material, another source was proposed, commonly referred to as "Q" (from the German word *Quelle*, meaning "source"), which Matthew and Luke each used in addition to Mark. This view is called the *two-source theory* (Mark and Q).

The nature of Q is hotly debated. Some say it was a single written source. Others say it was a variety of sources (written and oral). Some go so far as to reconstruct a "Q community" that produced this document and had its own unique theological perspective. This last proposal seems to be highly speculative, moving beyond the evidence.

Other Theories. Other scholars discount Q entirely. The *Farrer Hypothesis* (named after Austin Farrer, who wrote an influential article, "On Dispensing with Q," in 1955) accepts Markan priority but accounts for the material common to Matthew and Luke by asserting that Luke used Matthew in addition to Mark. The *Griesbach Hypothesis* (named after J. J. Griesbach, who popularized this view in the late eighteenth century) claims that Matthew wrote first, Luke used Matthew, and Mark abbreviated them both.

Despite continuing debates, the majority of New Testament scholars today hold to Markan priority, that Mark was the first Gospel written and that both Matthew and Luke used Mark. A smaller but still significant majority also affirm that Matthew and Luke had a common source (or sources), which is generally referred to as Q.

The two-source theory is sometimes referred to as the four-source theory, expanded to take account of the material unique to Matthew (called "M" or "Matthew's special material") and the material unique to Luke (called "L," or "Luke's special material").

FORM CRITICISM: SEEKING THE SPOKEN WORD BEHIND THE WRITTEN WORD

Form criticism (from the German *Formgeschichte*, "history of form") was developed in Germany in the early decades of the twentieth century. Its goal was to go behind the written sources and identify the earlier oral forms of the Gospel tradition.

Form critics operate from the assumption that between the time of Jesus and the writing of the Gospels, there was an oral period when the sayings and stories of Jesus were passed along by word of mouth. The technical term *pericope* (pronounced "pə-'ri-kə-pē") is used to identify each story, or unit of tradition.

Form critics identify these pericopes according to their "form." A form is a mini-genre, a particular type of story, such as a parable, a miracle story, or a wisdom saying. A pronouncement story is a short episode which introduces an authoritative pronouncement by Jesus (see Mark 2:14–17). The purpose of the story is to set up the pronouncement. Similarly, miracle stories are said to take certain, stereotypical forms, with a statement of the problem, followed by the miracle, followed by a reaction from onlookers.

The early church setting in which each form was used is called its *Sitz im Leben* (a German phrase meaning "setting in life"). Miracle stories may have been used in apologetic contexts, when Christians were defending the truth of Jesus' claims. Pronouncement stories may have been used as examples or illustrations in the preaching of the early church.

The goals of form criticism are (1) to classify and analyze forms, (2) to determine the church context in which each form originated and was used, and (3) to trace the history of a form's transmission in the church, how the form developed and was modified over time.

Form criticism was developed primarily as a historical tool to determine which sayings and stories could be traced to Jesus and which were developed and modified by the early church. Most early form critics assumed that the majority of the Gospel material had its origin in the preaching and teaching of the early church, rather than with the historical Jesus. Because form criticism's results concerning the historical Jesus have been mostly negative, some conservative scholars have rejected its use altogether.

Are there insights to be gained from form criticism? The answer is a qualified yes. The basic assumptions of form criticism are sound. Most of the Jesus tradition probably first circulated orally in small independent units, and these units were passed on in the context of the preaching and teaching of the church. Yet while the basic premise of form criticism is sound, the methodology has often been used to draw unwarranted conclusions. Many of the early form critics supposed that the early church had little interest in the historical Jesus and freely created most of the Gospel tradition. Historically, there has also been a strong antisupernatural bias, through which any supernatural elements in the Gospel tradition are viewed with suspicion.

In addition, the "forms" of the Gospel material are not as clear-cut as some form critics have supposed. Some pericopes do not fit well in any category, and others contain characteristics of more than one form. For example, the healing of the paralytic in Mark 2:1–12 contains features of both a miracle story and a pronouncement story. Some form critics attribute less historical value to such "mixed" forms. But this is unwarranted. Could not Jesus have healed a man and then made an authoritative pronouncement? So-called mixed forms tell us nothing one way or the other about the historicity of the material.

In short, while the first goal of form criticism—identifying the form or genre of individual Gospel stories—can provide illumination to the Gospel interpreter, the second two goals—identifying the setting and tracing the transmission—can be fraught with difficulties. Conclusions here tend to be highly subjective and speculative.

REDACTION CRITICISM: THE EVANGELISTS AS PURPOSEFUL EDITORS

Redaction criticism *(Redaktionsgeschichte)* arose in the middle of the twentieth century as a reaction against form criticism and its treatment of the Gospel writers as mere compilers of stories. It is recognized today that each Gospel writer is an author and a theologian in his own right. Redaction criticism looks at the work of these "redactors," or editors, and tries to determine why they collected, edited, and ordered the material the way they did.

The goals of redaction criticism are (1) to analyze how the Gospel writers "redacted," or edited, their sources, (2) to discern from this redaction the theological emphases of each writer, (3) to determine each author's purpose in writing, and (4) to identify the community situation, or setting in life *(Sitz im Leben)*, within which the author wrote. Here are some common patterns of redaction:

Summaries. A good indicator of an Evangelist's emphasis is the way he summarizes Jesus' activity. In Mark 1:45, the author notes that Jesus' popularity was so great he had to withdraw to the countryside. In his parallel, Luke makes a similar statement but gives an additional reason for Jesus' withdrawal: "Jesus often withdrew to lonely places and prayed" (Luke 5:16). Jesus' prayer life and his close communion with his Father are themes found frequently in Luke (Luke 3:21; 5:16; 6:12; 9:18, 28f.; 10:21f.; 11:1; 22:31f., 41ff.; 23:46).

Additions and Omissions of Material. Additions and omissions made to material can indicate an Evangelist's interests and purpose. For example, after the account of the Spirit's descent on Jesus at his baptism (Matt. 4:1; Mark 1:12–13), Luke alone adds that Jesus was "full of the Holy Spirit" when he was tempted by Satan in the wilderness (Luke 4:1–2). In both his Gospel and Acts, Luke places great emphasis on the role of the Holy Spirit in the life of Jesus and in the early church.

Arrangement of Material. Where an Evangelist places an episode may demonstrate his purpose and emphasis. Many scholars believe that the synagogue sermon in Luke 4:16–30 is the same sermon recorded in Mark 6:1–6, but that Luke has brought this episode forward as an introduction to and summary of Jesus' whole ministry.

Use of Additional Source Material. Luke includes many parables and stories that emphasize Jesus' special care for people of low estate, for sinners, and for society's outcasts, that are not found in the other Gospels (Luke 13:10–17; 14:7–14, 15–24; 15:7–10, 11–32; 16:19–31; 17:11–19; 18:9–14; 19:1–10). Luke's decision to include these stories shows his special interest in this theme.

Since most redaction critics have adopted Markan priority, the majority of redaction criticism has focused on how Matthew and Luke used Mark, Q, and their special material ("M" and "L"). Redaction criticism of Mark is more difficult since the sources he used are no longer available to us. Nevertheless, Mark's emphases can be determined by examining his editorial comments, summaries, transitions, and overall arrangement of material.

As with form criticism, the basic assumptions behind redaction criticism are sound. It is certain that the Evangelists used sources in writing their Gospels, and it is legitimate to ask how and why they used these sources the way they did. Redaction criticism also affirms that the Evangelists were purposeful writers and theologians.

Though the method as a whole is sound, redaction critics sometimes draw unwarranted conclusions. For example, many redaction critics too quickly assume that a saying or story found in only one Gospel was created by that writer. But *redaction* does not necessarily mean *creation*. Some redaction critics also find theological significance in every minor alteration made by the Evangelists. But such changes could be attributed to stylistic preference or to differences in sources.

A good corrective to this subjectivity is to keep an eye on the whole of the Gospel story, rather than only on its editorial alterations. This has led scholars to develop new methods that examine the Gospels as literary wholes. In appendix 2, we will examine one such method, narrative criticism.

Questions for Review and Discussion

1. Summarize the four stages that led to the production of the Gospels.
2. What is the synoptic problem and the most common solution?
3. What is redaction criticism? What are its goals, strengths, and weaknesses?

Recommended Resources

Porter, Stanley E., and Bryan R. Dyer, eds. *The Synoptic Problem: Four Views.* Grand Rapids: Baker, 2016.

Stein, Robert H. *Studying the Synoptic Gospels: Origin and Interpretation.* 2nd ed. Grand Rapids: Baker, 2001.

Synopsis of the Four Gospels. Revised Standard Version. Rev. ed. New York: American Bible Society, 2010.

THE GOSPELS AS STORY

Narrative Criticism

The methods of Gospel analysis discussed in appendix 1 (source, form, and redaction criticism) have been criticized for treating the Gospels as bits and pieces rather than as unified narratives. Narratives are stories, and stories are meant to be read and experienced from beginning to end.

While New Testament scholarship continues to benefit from these historical critical methods, Gospel studies have more and more turned from the *historical process* by which the Gospels arose, to their *present unity* as literary works. In this appendix, we will look at the most important of these methods, *narrative criticism*. Narrative critics have taken categories from modern literary criticism and applied them to the biblical text.

THE STORYTELLER

Narrative critics distinguish between the *real author*, the *implied author*, and the *narrator*. The real author is *the historical person who wrote the Gospel*. Though we can assume this person existed, the reader has no direct access to him. We may therefore speak of an implied author, *the literary version of the author as discerned in the text*. Though I cannot ask the writer of Mark's Gospel questions about the meaning of the text, I form an impression of the author's beliefs and worldview by following his narrative strategy.

A third category, the narrator, refers to *the voice we hear telling the story*. The narrator is not the real author or the implied author but a literary device that the implied author uses to tell the story. Different narratives have different kinds of narrators. The narrator may be outside the story, using the third person ("he," "she," "they"), or may be a character in the story, speaking in the first person ("I," "we"). In Mark Twain's classic *Huckleberry Finn*, Huck narrates the story in the first person, using the accent, grammar, and slang of a backwoods boy. With the exception of a few first-person passages in Acts (16:10–17; 20:5–15; 21:1–18; 27:1–28:16), the New Testament narratives always have third-person narrators. Third-person narrators may be omniscient and omnipresent, describing thoughts and events that no finite person could know. The narrator of Mark, for example, relates what the scribes are thinking (2:6–7) and recounts secret meetings behind closed doors (14:10–11).

NARRATIVE WORLD AND EVALUATIVE POINT OF VIEW

Closely related to the perspective of the narrator and implied author are the *narrative world* and the *evaluative point of view* of the narrative. The narrative world is the universe created by the implied author. "Created" does not mean that the setting has no counterpart in the real world. The Gospels are set in first-century Palestine. It means that in telling the story, the implied author "sets the stage" upon which the characters interact and the plot develops. Of course, the narrative world of the Gospels is not just first-century Palestine but also a supernatural universe inhabited by God, angels, Satan, and demons. Whether or not the reader believes in God, it is impossible to comprehend the story without entering this narrative world.

Evaluative point of view refers to the values, beliefs, and worldview that the reader is expected to adopt in order to judge the events and characters of the narrative. The Gospel narrators always affirm the evaluative point of view of God, who is righteous and just and loving. By contrast, Satan and his demons are deceitful, evil, and destructive. Characters in the story are presented as either good or bad depending on whether they follow the ways of God or the ways of Satan. For readers to comprehend the plot and track its narrative strategy, they must adopt the implied author's evaluative point of view.

THE STORY RECEIVER

Just as narrative critics distinguish between the real author, implied author, and narrator, so they distinguish between *real readers, implied readers*, and *narratees*. A real reader is any actual reader of the text, whether ancient or modern. The implied reader represents an imaginary person who responds appropriately to the narrative strategy. While an actual reader may respond to a text in a variety of ways, depending on their background and circumstances, the implied reader's response is predictable and dependent on the narrative strategy. When Judas betrays Jesus, the implied reader responds with dismay at this act of treachery. Yet in his classic missionary book *Peace Child*, Don Richardson describes a tribe in Papua New Guinea that considered deceit to be a virtue and so viewed Judas as the hero. In this case, real readers did not adopt the evaluative point of view of the narrative and so responded inappropriately to the implied author's strategy. The implied reader, by contrast, always responds appropriately so that the intention of the narrative is fulfilled.

Just as the narrator is the voice telling the story, so the narratee is the hearer of the story. Like the narrator, the narratee is a literary device used by the implied author to accomplish his purpose. While the narrator's voice is a constant feature of the Gospel narratives, only rarely is attention drawn to the narratee, as when the narrator in Luke addresses Theophilus (Luke 1:1–4) or when Mark's narrator pauses in the midst of Jesus' Olivet Discourse to comment, "Let the reader understand" (Mark 13:14).

PLOT: THE PROGRESS OF THE NARRATIVE

All stories have three fundamental components: *plot, setting*, and *characters*. Plot refers to the progress of the narrative, the sequence of events that move the story from introduction, to conflict, to climax, to resolution. Two fundamental features of plot are *causation* and *conflict*. Causation concerns the relationship of one scene to another. A plot progresses as one event leads to the next. Jesus' growing popularity in Mark is causally linked to the reports of his healing powers (Mark 1:45). The narrator in John makes the raising of Lazarus the decisive turning point that leads to Jesus' crucifixion (John 11:45–57).

Conflict is common to all narrative. It comes early in Mark's Gospel as Jesus is tempted by Satan in the desert (1:12). The narrator signals by this that the story is not a merely human struggle but a spiritual conflict. This is confirmed as Jesus immediately comes into conflict with a demon-possessed man in the synagogue at Capernaum (1:21–25). These spiritual encounters set the stage for his conflicts with the religious leaders (2:1–3:34). By juxtaposing these episodes, the narrator portrays the religious leaders as allies of Satan in opposition to God.

While conflict is common to all four Gospels, it develops in different ways and to different degrees. Matthew paints an extremely negative portrait of the religious leaders as evil and unredeemable opponents of Jesus. Luke provides a more mixed view. Jesus socializes with Pharisees (Luke 7:36; 11:37; 14:1) and is even warned by them of Herod's schemes (13:31). This sets the stage for Acts, where the religious leaders are given a second chance to respond (Acts 3:17–19) and where the Pharisees show some affinity with the Christian movement (5:33–39; 15:5; 23:7–9).

Another important feature of plot relates to time and sequence. *Story time* concerns the passage of time in the narrative world of the text. Story time may move quickly, as when the narrator summarizes Jesus' activity of preaching and healing throughout Galilee (Matt. 9:35). Here a single sentence summarizes weeks or even months. Story time may stop, as the narrator provides an explanation or makes a comment (Mark 7:3–4). It may jump forward days, months, or years (twenty years from Luke 2:51 to 3:1) or back to a previous time (Mark 6:14–29). The speed with which story time is narrated may indicate an author's emphasis. In Matthew's Gospel, Jesus often teaches in long discourses in which the narration runs at approximately the same speed as story time (Matthew 5–7). This slowing emphasizes Jesus' role in Matthew as a great, Moses-like teacher. In all four Gospels, story time slows considerably during the last week of Jesus' life and particularly through the passion narrative. This reveals how important Jesus' death was for the Evangelists.

CHARACTERS

Closely related to the plot are its *characters*, whose actions and interactions carry the narrative forward. Characters can be individuals, like

Peter, Nicodemus, and Judas. Or they can be groups, like the disciples, the Pharisees, or the crowds. Groups function as characters when they share similar traits and act together in the narrative. When the crowd shouts for Jesus' death—"Crucify him!" (Mark 15:13)— they are functioning as a single character.

Characterization is the manner in which characters are portrayed. Characters are understood from their *traits*, qualities attributed to them in the narrative. These traits may emerge through *telling* or *showing*. Telling is when the narrator explicitly ascribes a trait to the character. Zechariah and Elizabeth, the parents of John the Baptist, are described as "righteous in the sight of God" (Luke 1:6). Showing is when a character's traits emerge indirectly through their words and actions. John the Baptist's righteous character is revealed in Matthew through his preaching and baptizing ministry (3:1–17), Jesus' testimony to his greatness (11:7–19), and the events surrounding his martyrdom (14:1–12).

Literary critics distinguish various types of characters. *Round characters* are complex and often unpredictable, with multiple traits. *Flat characters* are simple, one-dimensional, and predictable. Peter is a classic round character, with his contradictory traits of impetuous zeal, extreme loyalty, and wavering faith. The religious leaders are generally flat, predictably self-righteous, envious, and hypocritical.

This brings up the relationship of characterization to evaluative point of view. Characters are either good or bad, right or wrong, depending on their relationship to the story's evaluative point of view. Jesus is the main character and protagonist because he reflects perfectly the evaluative point of view of God. The chief antagonists— Satan, demons, and the religious leaders—oppose Jesus and so run counter to God's purpose and plan.

SETTING

Setting refers to all facets of the narrative world in which characters act and events occur. There are three kinds of setting: local, temporal, and social-cultural.

Local setting refers to any spatial orientation, whether geography (mountains, lakes, etc.), political-cultural locales (Galilee, Judea,

Jerusalem), or any other object or place (a room, a boat, a manger). Settings often carry symbolic as well as historical significance. Mountains are places of revelation, especially in Matthew's Gospel, in which Jesus is presented as a kind of new Moses giving God's law on the mountain (Matt. 5:1). Jerusalem plays an important symbolic role in Luke's Gospel and the book of Acts. It is the place where God's salvation is accomplished and from where the message of salvation goes forth (Acts 1:8). But it also represents Israel's stubborn rejection of God's purpose and her coming judgment (Luke 13:34).

Temporal settings also appear throughout the Gospels. Many of these are general ("one day Jesus was teaching" [Luke 5:17]); others are more specific. Jesus' transfiguration occurs "after six days" (Mark 9:2), and he dies "at three in the afternoon" (Mark 15:34). Temporal settings, like physical ones, can carry symbolic significance. The forty days of Jesus' testing in the wilderness are analogous to Israel's forty years of wandering. In John, Jesus' teaching during various Jewish festivals often carries symbolic links to those festivals. Jesus identifies himself as the "light of the world" and offers "living water" to the thirsty while teaching at the Feast of Tabernacles, a festival marked by water-pouring and lamp-lighting ceremonies (John 7:2, 37–39; 8:12).

Social-cultural setting refers to the world of human relationships in which the narrative occurs. These settings may be political, social, cultural, or economic. The Gospel narratives take place during the Roman occupation of Palestine in the first century AD. Jesus' statement "Give back to Caesar what is Caesar's" (Mark 12:17 par.) makes little sense without an awareness of Roman authority and the Jewish revolutionary movements that arose from it. Jesus' parable of the tenant farmers (Mark 12:1–12 par.) comes to life when we recognize, first, that it is an adaptation of Isaiah's parable of the vineyard (Isa. 5:1–7) and, second, that it has as its backdrop the economic realities of poor peasant farmers in the Galilean countryside.

ASSESSMENT OF NARRATIVE CRITICISM

Narrative criticism is a useful tool that provides important correctives to historical-critical methods. Most important, narrative criticism reads the text according to its literary form—as narrative, or story. The Gospel writers intentionally chose narrative as their medium, utilizing plot, characters, and settings to pass on the significance of Jesus.

Narrative criticism also respects the unity and integrity of the text, focusing on its present form rather than on the oral traditions or hypothetical sources that lie behind it. Narrative analysis has confirmed that the Evangelists were indeed authors and literary artists, not just compilers of traditions.

There are also some potential weaknesses of narrative criticism. In using categories associated with novels, narrative critics sometimes assume the nonhistoricity of the text, treating "story" as synonymous with "fiction." Narrative critics also sometimes ignore or avoid historical and cultural background. Since authors create narrative worlds, it is sometimes assumed that historical and cultural backgrounds are of little significance. But this wrongly assumes that narrative worlds have no relationship to the real world. The more readers know about this background, the better they will understand the story.

A third potential weakness is that narrative critics sometimes ignore or reject historical-critical approaches. Yet while source and redaction criticism go beyond the scope of narrative criticism, they are not incompatible with it, and the methods can be used together. The likelihood that the Gospel writers used each other as sources means we can gain insights through their comparison.

Questions for Review and Discussion

1. What is the goal of narrative criticism?
2. What is the difference between a real author, an implied author, and a narrator?
3. What does "evaluative point of view" mean? What is the evaluative point of view of the Gospels?
4. Describe the main features of plot, characterization, and setting.

Recommended Resources

Powell, Mark Allen. *What Is Narrative Criticism?* Guides to Biblical Scholarship. Minneapolis: Fortress, 1991.

Resseguie, James L. *Narrative Criticism of the New Testament: An Introduction.* Grand Rapids: Baker, 2005.

Rhoads, David, Joanna Dewey, and Donald Michie. *Mark as Story: An Introduction to the Narrative of a Gospel.* 3rd ed. Philadelphia: Fortress, 2012.

SUBJECT INDEX

Aaron, 32
Abraham, 26, 39–40, 42, 101
Acts, book of, 62–63, 70–71. *See also* Luke, Gospel of
Adam, 101, 114
Alexander the Great, 18–19
Anna, 66, 74
Antioch, 19, 37
Antiochus, 19–20, 30, 136
anti-Semitism, 46–47, 138
apocalyptic literature, 117
apocryphal gospels, 16
apologetics, 36, 51, 156
apostles, 58, 94–95, 132–33, 148–49
atonement theology, 141, 143
authentic faith, 34

Babylonian Empire, 18, 39–40
banquet parable, 68
baptism, 110–11, 112–13
Barabbas, 138
Beatitudes, 73, 121
Beloved Disciple, 78, 82, 98
Bethlehem, 103–4
birth narrative, 66–67, 71, 72, 73, 104–6
Book of Acts in the Setting of Hellenistic History (Hemer), 93
bread of life, 83

Caesar Augustus, 22, 23, 104, 138–39
Caiaphas, 28
cause-and-effect relationships, 123
census, 104
Christianity, 11

Christianity *(continued)*
  goal of, 60
  impact of destruction of Jerusalem on, 25
  and Qumran community, 32
  spread of, 23
Christology, 10, 85
  John's, 99
  Luke's, 73
  Matthew's, 43
Clement of Alexandria, 50, 77
conception, virginal, 102–3
contrasts, 80
covenant, 26, 42
crucifixion. *See* death, Jesus'

David, 32, 39–40, 42, 101, 103, 133
Day of Atonement, 28
dead, raising, 127
Dead Sea Scrolls, 78, 110
death, 61
  defeat of, 150
  Jesus', 14, 82, 138–44
  sacrificial, 120, 137
deism, 123
Diatessaron, 14
Didache, 37
dietary laws, 27, 30, 55, 119
disciples and discipleship, 46, 58–59, 68, 120–21, 132
divine sovereignty, 73
dualism, Johannine, 78, 88–89

Egypt, 19, 105
Elizabeth, 66, 72, 74, 109
end-times resurrection, 127, 149, 150
end-times salvation, 70, 72, 75, 117

SCRIPTURE INDEX

Four Portraits, One Jesus

A Survey of Jesus and the Gospels

Mark L. Strauss

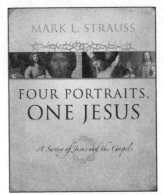

To Christians worldwide, the man Jesus of Nazareth is the centerpiece of history, the object of faith, hope, and worship. Even those who do not follow him admit the vast influence of his life. For anyone interested in knowing more about Jesus, study of the four biblical Gospels is essential. *Four Portraits, One Jesus* is a thorough yet accessible introduction to these documents and their subject, the life and person of Jesus. Like different artists rendering the same subject using different styles and points of view, the Gospels paint four highly distinctive portraits of the same remarkable Jesus. With clarity and insight, Mark Strauss illuminates these four books, first addressing their nature, origin, methods for study, and historical, religious, and cultural backgrounds. He then moves on to closer study of each narrative and its contribution to our understanding of Jesus, investigating things such as plot, characters, and theme. Finally, he pulls it all together with a detailed examination of what the Gospels teach about Jesus' ministry, message, death, and resurrection, with excursions into the quest for the historical Jesus and the historical reliability of the Gospels.

Available in stores and online!

Four Portraits, One Jesus Video Lectures

A Survey of Jesus and the Gospels

Mark L. Strauss

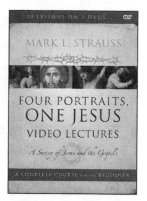

Four Portraits, One Jesus Video Lectures features twenty lessons (on three DVDs) and provides a full overview of Jesus' life and ministry from top New Testament scholar Mark Strauss.

A companion to the widely used textbook *Four Portraits, One Jesus*, these lectures are an ideal resource for students and independent learners who want an additional contact point with the material from the textbook to enhance their studies.

Introducing the New Testament

A Short Guide to Its History and Message

D. A. Carson, Douglas J. Moo,
edited by Andrew David Naselli

This book focuses on historical questions dealing with authorship, date, sources, purpose, and destination of the New Testament books. By focusing on the essentials, the authors ensure that each book is accurately understood within its historical settings. For each New Testament document, the authors also provide a summary of that book's content and discuss the book's theological contribution to the overall canon. This abridgement includes questions at the end of each chapter to facilitate group discussion and personal review. It will help a new generation of students and church leaders better grasp the message of the New Testament.

Available in stores and online!

Introducing the Old Testament

A Short Guide to Its History and Message

Tremper Longman III

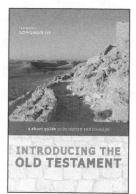

An abridged edition of the bestselling book *An Introduction to the Old Testament*, this rich guide makes Old Testament scholarship accessible to the average reader. Renowned Bible scholar Tremper Longman III gathers the best in historical research and literary analysis to lead the reader through each book of the Old Testament. Most significant, Longman explores the meaning of each book in light of its cultural setting. Abbreviated chapters highlight key research discoveries, ensuring that the information is both significant and manageable. Including questions at the end of each chapter for group discussion or personal reflection, *Introducing the Old Testament* makes the words, history, and culture of biblical times come alive for readers. Laypersons as well as church leaders will take away a solid understanding of the historical background and theological message of the Old Testament and be inspired to apply biblical truths to their lives.

Available in stores and online!

Introducing Christian Ethics

A Short Guide to Making Moral Choices

Scott B. Rae

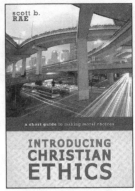

Introducing Christian Ethics helps Christians form a sound basis for making ethical decisions in today's complex postmodern world. Raising fourteen key ethical questions on today's most pressing issues, including abortion, war, sexual ethics, capital punishment, and more, Scott Rae guides his readers in making moral choices wisely.

Based on the bestselling college and seminary ethics textbook *Moral Choices*, this book distills nearly two decades of teaching and study into a succinct and user-friendly volume. It is an ideal primer for pastors, students, and everyday Christians who desire engagement with the world around them in an intelligent and informed manner.

Teaching and study resources for the book, including additional video clips based on the questions corresponding to each chapter, make it ideal for use in the classroom as well as for pastors and for teaching settings within the church. Resources are available through www.ZondervanAcademic.com.

Available in stores and online!

Journey into God's Word

Your Guide to Understanding and Applying the Bible

J. Scott Duvall and J. Daniel Hays

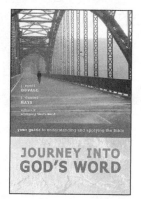

Life is a journey, and like any journey, it requires an accurate, reliable roadmap to get us where we need to go. God has provided such a guide in his Word. But just as a navigator needs to learn how to interpret all the contours and symbols of a map, so also we need to be able to understand how the Bible communicates its directions to us. *Journey Into God's Word* helps Bible readers acquire these skills and become better at reading, interpreting, and applying the Bible to life. This abridgment of the bestselling college/seminary textbook *Grasping God's Word* takes the proven principles from that book and makes them accessible to people in the church. It starts with general principles of interpretation, then applies them to specific genres and contexts. Hands-on exercises guide readers through the interpretation process, with an emphasis on real-life application.

Available in stores and online!

Christian Beliefs

Twenty Basics Every Christian Should Know

Wayne A. Grudem,
edited by Elliot Grudem

God doesn't call every Christian to go off to seminary, but there are certain matters of doctrine—the church's teaching—that every Christian simply must know. Theology is important because what we believe affects how we live. If you're a relatively new believer in Jesus, or if you're a more mature Christian looking for a quick brush-up on basics of the faith, *Christian Beliefs* is for you. This readable guide to twenty basic Christian beliefs is a condensation of Wayne Grudem's award-winning book on systematic theology, prized by pastors and teachers everywhere. He and his son, Elliot, have boiled down the essentials of Christian theology for the average layperson and made them both clear and applicable to life. You will learn about the Bible, the characteristics of God, what it means that we are created in the image of God, what God has done for us in Christ, the purpose of the church, and much more. Each chapter includes questions for personal review or group discussion.

Available in stores and online!